SUCCESS FOR KIDS

IN

ACTIVE GAMES

Steven A. Henkel, Ph.D.
Bethel University

ISBN 978-1-4507-1401-3

CREDITS

Instructional technology consultants: Betsy Dadabo and Calvin Konop

Illustrators: Adam Turner and Brandon Wind

Cover design: BRIO Publishing

Printer: MGB Printing

Direct inquiries and orders to:

Steven Henkel
Professor, Bethel University
www.bethel.edu/~shenkel/books.html
active.games4u@gmail.com

Printed in the United States of America

Dedication

Appreciate kids who are different
Who try, but flounder in games,
Who miss a big pass,
Then run out of gas,
And make no halls of fame.

If only kids could be different
And still succeed in games,
They'd try even more,
Whatever the score,
And learn to value their names.

Success is intended to be
For all who are swift or lame,
Not measured by points,
Or strength of the joints,
But effort put forth in the game.

This book is dedicated to the children who are different—children who fail in traditional active games—children who could succeed if someone would redefine success—children who could learn to value themselves for who they are in God's eyes, instead of for what they can do.

Contents

Preface: Another side of games   vii

Acknowledgments   xi

Part I • Game Challenges and Choices   xiii

   Chapter 1: Elements of a game   1

      Goals   3
      Alignment   3
      Movements   5
      Equipment   6
      Social structure   7

   Chapter 2: Game elements and self-esteem   11

      Self-esteem building blocks   11
      "Arranging the blocks"   13

   Chapter 3: Competition *and* cooperation   25

      Assumptions about competition   25
      Monitoring the way we compete   28
      Monitoring the extent of our competitiveness   32

Part II • Game Choices in Process   35

Chapter 4: Games for partners   37

Chapter 5: Games for small groups   55

Chapter 6: Games for large groups   97

Chapter 7: Relay games   137

Chapter 8: Game administration   161

      Pregame responsibilities   161
      Game responsibilities   164
      Postgame responsibilities   168

Closing   171

Bibliography   173

Index   177

National standards for physical education   180

About the author   181

Preface

Another Side of Games

..."We now return to our regularly scheduled traditional competitive game, where *Effort* is attempting to become 'King of the Mountain"
...There he goes, fans! Let's all watch *Effort* as he tries to scale that wall of snow. In order to be 'King of the Mountain' he must make it to the top. Many others have made it, so we can expect the same from him...

...It looks like *Effort* is trying the right side first...He's making some progress, though slower than the others...He'll soon be to the first obstacle. It's going to be difficult getting around that large snowbank. He'll need to grip tightly...There's one handhold...and another...I think he made it...Yes! Now on to the next snowbank...He's leaning into the hill...Oh no! He's been pushed down the side by *Aggressive*! I'm sure he won't let that discourage him. He can withstand a couple of bumps...

...Now *Effort* is going to try the left side...He's climbing diagonally to the outside. He'll have to get over a large dip in the snowbank...Here comes the jump...*Effort* is taking to the air...It's not a very high take-off. He'll need to sail far in order to have a chance...Whoops; one leg did not make it. I believe that *Rut* has trapped his leg. If he can just pull it out he might be able to...Yes! The leg is free, but now he's rolling down the hill out of control—a few more bruises for the lad, but nothing he can't handle...

...*Effort* is moving up once again. If only he can make it to the top...I hope he sees the icy spot coming up. Making it over this obstacle would be a key turning point. Maybe *Effort* can gain some confidence for the remainder of the climb...He's trying to dig in his boot...definitely showing a lot of determination...He's part way over the ice...Now *Effort* is reaching with the other foot...just a little farther...Oh no! Down he goes again. I'm afraid *Slick* has gotten the best of him this time. Wow, does he look discouraged. I'm not sure how much longer *Effort* can go on..."

How much longer can a child or adolescent like *Effort* actually endure failure? Perhaps not very long. What is the cost of a child enduring failure time after time? The 'King of the Mountain' metaphor could reflect a child's experience in a variety of physical activities, but particularly the experience of unskilled players in traditional competitive games. Kids try to meet the challenge at hand, whether it be catching a ball or running to a base. They make some progress, but are seldom successful because they cannot perform as well as the expectation. Someone inevitably "shoves them back down the mountain."

So, unskilled children begin the climb again and the cycle repeats itself. Kids make it around one obstacle and perhaps, a second. They may overcome some physical bumps and emotional bruises for a short while, but again success is out of view. Why is success so elusive? It is unattainable because the children have too narrow of perspective. No one taught them to view success as doing their best first of all, and as overcoming one obstacle at a time second of all. Instead, many kids are taught that success is achieved by "getting all the way to the top." Children who fail over and over have wounded self-esteems and eventually give up.

In the metaphor, *Effort* tried scaling the right and left sides of the mountain. Is there another side of the mountain—another side of active games in general, where all children can be successful? Indeed there is and kids need help to climb it. Some educators believe forsaking competition altogether is necessary to eliminate widespread failure. I disagree. Instead, children can experience success in active games through three avenues: alternative competitive games, cooperative games, and independent games.

The book promotes values that are universal, or applicable to any setting—game ideas that will benefit leaders and children not only in schools, but in home schools, churches, camps and other community settings. Biblical references are included for leaders in Christian education programs, including those who prepare leaders in Christian higher education.

Part I of the book reveals common elements of games, as well as challenges associated with the different game avenues. Each of the challenges may be overcome by making choices that include, rather than exclude, players. Being included is critical to the development of a child's self-esteem. Additional aspects of character development through game play are addressed in a complementary book (Henkel, 2010). With so many negative role models in the sports media, the need for promoting positive values has never been more acute.

Part II provides game leaders with 94 inclusive games to use in a variety of educational settings with elementary and middle school age children. Leaders are encouraged to try the games provided, and to use the ideas to generate more games of their own. For people with limited experience leading recreational activities, Part II includes a chapter on selected "how to's" of administrating games.

Games in each chapter are sequenced by the recommended ages of participants. A range is provided for each game, beginning as young as age five and extending as old as age 14 and up. An index lists games by chapter in the order presented (see p. 177). The index also indicates the national standards for physical education best addressed by each activity (see p. 180). The national standards correspond to important outcomes for physical activity identified by the National Association for Sport and Physical Education (NASPE, 2004). Note that while the index highlights Standards 1, 2, 4, and 5, Standards 3 and 6 may be addressed by most any game, depending on the emphasis and dialogue provided by leaders.

Throughout the book success is defined as "doing one's best in accomplishing a task." Whether playing games, writing a poem, or washing dishes, doing one's best requires having a pure motive (1 Samuel 17:46; Proverbs 16:3), appropriating skill (Ecclesiastes 10:10), and valuing help from others (Proverbs 15:22). A given task may or may not actually require help from others, and it may or may not involve an opponent. Although success requires appropriating skill, its ultimate realization also involves divine intervention or oversight. A person needs to seek the Lord (1 Samuel 14:47; 2 Chronicles 26:5) and recognize that his grace makes task completion possible. Otherwise, a person's efforts are in vain (Psalm 127:1-2).

Acknowledgments

I appreciate the assistance of committed friends and family in writing this book. Colleagues in the Bethel University library helped me secure valuable resources and navigate the word processing to prepare the text and graphic images. Betsy Dadabo and Calvin Konop were particularly helpful, with no indication that my frequent interruptions were a bother. Adam Turner and Brandon Wind drew unique sketches of games, and BRIO Publishing designed the cover with grant money provided by the Bethel University Alumni Board. I also appreciate the blurbs written by Curt Hinson and Dan Midura to help communicate the value of the book to others. Thanks to each of you for sharing your expertise.

This book could not have been written without the patience and support of my family. Brad, Trent, and Craig have been my primary playmates during their formidable years. My interactions with them, and on behalf of them with respect to games, have helped shape my ideas. Thank you especially, Vicki, for being my greatest "cheerleader," especially when progress was slow.

A final word of thanks goes to the many elementary and middle school children who endured the piloting of games. Every game did not work the first time. Some games evolved because children were willing to try something new, and because they were patient when I made adjustments "on the spot." Let this be an encouragement to readers who make up or modify your own games.

Part I

Game Challenges and Choices

Active games present challenges to leaders. Leaders need to select games for children and adolescents from a vast assortment available. Children may or may not succeed in a game because they range so much in developmental level and in skills acquired. Even when a game is appropriately chosen, leaders have the challenge of understanding all the elements involved and how to explain them to players. Each of these challenges is addressed in Part I.

In chapter 1 the elements of a game are closely examined. Understanding general aspects of play and specific game elements helps leaders match a game with a particular purpose or reason for playing. Leaders will also gain a better understanding of the challenges associated with different social structures within games.

Chapter 2 considers the relationship of social structure and other elements to self-esteem. The chapter answers questions such as, "What are the building blocks of self-esteem"? and "How can I include all kids in a game"? Leaders are presented with choices for changing games to meet the needs of children of all ability levels. In the case of competitive games, the choices have to do with monitoring the way people compete and the extent of their competitiveness. This is the subject of chapter 3.

Chapter 1

Elements of a Game

R ecreational games involving physical activity provide a primary
way for children and youth to interact with, and learn from, their
world. Games offer opportunities to practice motor skills, learn
social values, and shape personal identity. In addition to a game's
outcomes, the nature of a game may be defined by describing what people
do during the game—play, and by describing specific elements that
comprise a game.

Classic works on play suggest some general aspects common to all
play forms. These aspects are captured by Huizinga (1955), who
describes play in the following manner:

> ...a free activity standing quite consciously outside 'ordinary' life
> as being 'not serious,' but at the same time absorbing the player
> intensely and utterly. It is an activity connected with no material
> interest, and no profit can be gained by it. It proceeds within its
> own proper boundaries of time and space...(p. 13).

According to Huizinga, play is first of all free, or **voluntary**. A person
enters into play by an act of her own free will. Play occurs during leisure
time and so may be deferred or suspended at any time. It is not a task to
be done by an individual, nor is it imposed on a person as an obligation or
duty. Organized sport, then, does not represent play in its truest sense,

since a player's will is bound by commitment to the team.

A second general aspect of play is its nonordinary, or **unreal** nature. It involves escaping or removing oneself from normal life. Sometimes escape occurs directly, as in make believe play. The thing or situation being played out does not actually exist in real life. Common play characters of this kind include a pirate or princess. Most of the time escape from normal life is indirect. Even though players do not make believe in typical recreational games, they may escape from normal life in the sense that all other concerns are potentially left behind.

Thirdly, play is **pleasing**, an end in itself. It is entered into for enjoyment. Activities pursued with material gain in mind, such as prizes or trophies, are not considered true play. Although Huizinga acknowledges that material purposes may be accomplished indirectly through play, the intrinsic value of play provides reason enough to participate.

The remaining aspect of play is its **secludedness**. Play forms are bound by limits of space and time. Spatial limitations include the setting and boundaries. Settings range from a playground to a back yard outdoors, and from a gymnasium to a hallway indoors. Sometimes a play space is further limited by boundaries within the setting, such as lines or markers.

The size and shape of boundaries are critical to accomplishing a game's goal(s). A game that incorporates continuous chasing, such as *Chain Tag* (p. 123), requires a large enough area to spread out players in order to move optimally. By contrast, the game *Dribble Tag* (p. 125) is only effective when players are kept in close proximity. Too large a space limits interaction between players. Whatever the setting and/or boundaries, play occurs within a temporary world. Although a game may be repeated frequently, a single occurrence has a definite beginning and is confined to a relatively clear time frame.

Aspects of play described here are helpful in understanding the nature of a game. The aspects are not all encompassing, however, since all games involve play, but not all forms of play occur in games. Therefore, the nature of a game may also be characterized by more specific elements. The elements of a game may be described using the "GAMES" acronym (Henkel, 1995). Each element in the acronym contains particular examples that distinguish one game from another:

G = Goals
A = Alignment
M = Movements
E = Equipment
S = Social structure

Goals

The first common element of games is their educational value. While the intrinsic value of play is clear, this book is written primarily to promote educational ends achieved through play. Children can have fun and learn something too. Children may fulfill the need to play for its own sake when they are merely supervised, rather than guided, by adults, or when they are unsupervised altogether. The distinction, then, is between the adult roles of guiding and supervising activities. Often children are supervised during recess, at the neighborhood playground, or in their yards. Adult presence is more for insuring safety, than for initiating meaningful play ideas.

On the other hand, adults are responsible to guide children in their play choices while in the role of an educator. Serving as a guide requires a thorough understanding of alternative goals and how they may be achieved, a challenge to be sure. While the role of an educator is obvious in the school or home school setting, leaders in youth sports and other community programs may also serve primarily as teachers. Although games in this book are physical in nature, alternative goals extend beyond practicing motor skills or improving fitness. Other goals may be social, intellectual, or even spiritual in nature. Social goals include communicating with others and displaying leadership. Intellectual goals include learning particular concepts and solving problems.

Spiritual goals involving character development are the least common of all goals within games. Aspects of character to target in games include diligence, humility and self-control. Specific ways to address these and other virtues are contained in a complimentary book, *Integrating Active Games with Other Subjects* (Henkel, 2010).

Alignment

Every game has an alignment, or way that players are arranged spatially. While not exhaustive, Figure 1.1 depicts several examples. Common examples include geometrical shapes (i.e. Alignments a, b, and c in Figure 1.1). Players within alignments may be connected, as shown in Alignment a in the figure. Arrangement of players may also change during the course of a game. Change does not occur in *Fruit of the Room* (p. 69), depicted by Alignment b. Player alignment does change in *Rhythmical Red Light* (p. 102), in which people initially stand on one line, then move in scatter arrangement to the other line (i.e. Alignment d). Since game alignment can change, all alignments described via the GAMES acronym throughout the book represent initial positions of

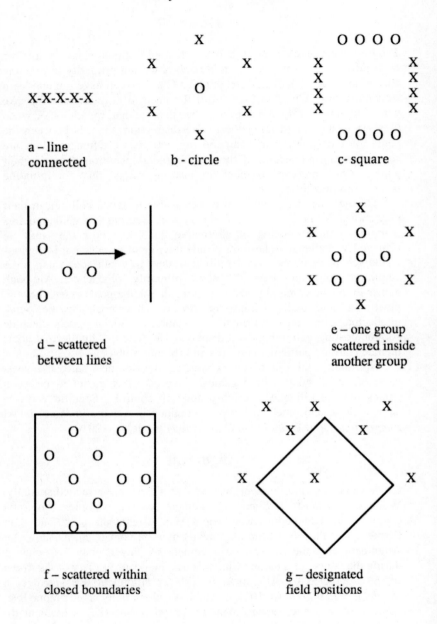

Figure 1.1: Examples of player alignments.

players. In addition to player alignments changing, more than one alignment may occur simultaneously. For instance, one group of players may be scattered inside another group of players who form a geometrical shape (i.e. Alignment e).

Although players may be scattered in no recognizable shape, the boundaries of a game may form a shape around players, as depicted by Alignment f. The final alignment illustrated in Figure 1.1 shows players in designated field positions (i.e. Alignment g). Locations of designated positions are based on the number and experience of players, as well as the motor skills performed.

Movements

Games described in this book involve physical exercise. Exercise may directly target motor skills or fitness, and/or may be used to help accomplish nonphysical goals. Either way, all games provided involve some large muscle movements unlike more sedentary games, such as dressing up in adult clothes or playing a video game.

Learners use a variety of motor skills or patterns while playing games. Four classifications of motor skills are represented in Table 1.1. Classifications include (a) locomotor patterns, (b) nonlocomotor patterns, (c) object control skills, and (d) sport skills.

Table 1.1

Examples of Motor Skills by Classification

LOCOMOTOR PATTERNS		NONLOCOMOTOR PATTERNS	
Galloping	Running	Bending	Stretching
Hopping	Skipping	Curling	Swaying
Jumping	Sliding	Rocking	Turning
Leaping	Walking	Spinning	Twisting

OBJECT CONTROL SKILLS		SPORT SKILLS	
Bouncing	Rolling	Batting	Pitching
Catching	Striking	Bowling	Punting
Collecting	Swinging	Fielding	Serving
Dribbling	Throwing	High jumping	Spiking
Kicking	Tossing	Long jumping	Volleying

Locomotor patterns involve moving the body from place to place, normally on one's feet, as in galloping or running. Nonlocomotor patterns consist of actions the body does in place, such as bending or stretching. Sport skills are distinguished from object control skills and locomotor patterns based on the complexity of the situation. Games involving object control may require players to throw or strike a ball in a basic sense, whereas games with sport skills might require players to utilize the throw and strike in the form of a pitch or spike, respectively. The latter examples involve precision and accuracy not required of basic skills. Likewise, when a game requires players to perform a long jump for maximum distance, the movement is considered a complex sport skill, rather than a basic locomotor pattern.

Skills utilized in games may be chosen by game leaders or by players. Allowing input from players is one way to match skills to their interests and developmental levels. Another way is to provide alternatives within the same game. Game alternatives and other developmental considerations are discussed in more detail in chapter 2.

Equipment

Equipment may be the most familiar aspect of games. Equipment represents (a) spatial boundaries on the floor or ground, (b) spatial boundaries in the air, (c) items used with patterns of locomotion and nonlocomotion, (d) items used in object control or sport skill tasks, and (e) items worn on the body. Spatial boundaries on the floor or ground are commonly marked with bases, cones, polydots or tape. Markers must be chosen to fit the environmental conditions. In general, indoor markers can be short, lightweight and fewer in number when permanent lines are present. Outdoor markers generally need to be taller, heavier and more plentiful. Markers with these specifications withstand the wind and uneven ground, and increase visibility.

Spatial boundaries in the air include a net, rope or wall. Walls are dangerous boundaries in games, particularly if players advance toward them. Instead, leaders should enforce stringent boundaries inside the walls. A wall can serve as an effective target, however, as long as equipment, rather than players contact the wall.

A variety of equipment may be used to enhance locomotor and nonlocomotor patterns. With locomotor patterns equipment often serves as a spatial reference point or as an obstacle. In *Chain Tag* (p. 123), a hoop or tire serves as a reference point for the tagger to return to intermittently. During *Invent a Course* (p. 72), cones, tires and other equipment serve as obstacles for players to go around, over or through. Equipment used with nonlocomotor patterns includes beanbags, hoops, wands and scarves. Equipment may be balanced on the body, as in *Heads Up* (p. 100), or manipulated by the body, as in *Loop da Hoop* (p. 58).

Items used in object control or sports skill tasks are similar to those used with locomotor and nonlocomotor patterns. Balls and rackets are common examples. Items need to be chosen with safety and the nature of the learning environment in mind. When considering safety, the longer and heavier a racket, the more spacing required between players. The smaller and heavier a ball, the less throwing velocity permitted in a game. With regard to the environment, the windy outdoors requires different object control equipment than a protected gymnasium. A game that utilizes a wiffle ball indoors may require a tennis ball outdoors.

Items worn on the body consist of flags and pinnies. Velcro flags are preferred for tagging games to clarify who is and who is not tagged. On the other hand, pinnies or jerseys can be more visibly seen in games that distinguish teams.

As with other game elements, flexibility with equipment is key in achieving stated goals. Criteria for determining developmental appropriateness of equipment is discussed in chapter 2.

Social Structure

The social structure of a game involves the number of players or groups of players in a game, as well as the way in which players or groups relate to one another. Game leaders have three choices for relationships among players: competitive, cooperative or independent. Midura and Glover (1999) describe three models for a competitive social structure. The viability of a military model, in which opponents are enemies, is dismissed on biblical grounds elsewhere (Henkel, 2007). The definition of competition used here draws from the other two models.

Competition is defined as a contest in which one person or team strives with another person or team (or multiple teams) to achieve a mutually exclusive outcome. The idea of "striving with" comes from the Latin word *–petere,* meaning "to strive," and the prefix *com-,* meaning "with." The outcome is mutually exclusive, because declaring a winner comes at the expense of one or more losers. Competition may occur between two individuals (i.e. *Table Tennis*), within a single group (i.e. *Four Square*), or between two or more groups (i.e. *Volleyball*). Competition may be classified as a "zero sum" activity when victory results in one loser, and a "negative sum" activity when victory results in more than one loser (Brown & Grineski, 1992, p. 22). This description of competition encompasses aspects of a reward model, since players strive to gain points, prizes or other recognition that are in limited supply, and also a partnership model, since the quest for rewards may be more a function of the structure of a contest, than of the players' attitudes. The most advantageous attitudes view opponents as facilitators of, rather than obstacles to, one's own performance (Fraleigh, 1984). Midura and Glover (1999) portray the reward and partnership models as mutually exclusive, whereas they may actually co-exist. Their co-existence is clarified here in chapter 3 in the context of distinguishing between structural and intentional competition.

Professionals debate whether competition can involve just one individual—whether a person could theoretically compete against himself and/or against "the elements." Contests of this kind provide challenge without comparing individuals. Although individual activities are important for rounding out a person's skill development and games participation, the debate is beyond the scope of this book. Since *Success for Kids in Active Games* intentionally addresses group games, all references to competition involve two or more individuals.

In contrast to a traditional competitive game, a cooperative game is characterized by mutually compatible goals. The success of one player or team contributes to the success of other players or teams. Rewards are not limited because all participants potentially share in obtaining those available. In *Clockwise Four Square* (p. 57), rewards consist of cumulative group hits or points. Players cooperate by striking a ball the most number of consecutive times as a group, instead of compete by trying to get others "out." More experienced players can strike the ball with their nondominant hands only and/or hit the ball as many times as possible in a given period of time.

Aspects of competitive and cooperative social structures may be contained in the same game. When the predominant social structure is characterized by competition between different teams, players within the same team may potentially cooperate with one another. Cooperation within competition may also occur when individuals try to defeat one small group, as in the game *Let My People Go* (Henkel, 2010, p. 95), or when small groups try to defeat one individual, as in the game *Chain Tag* (p. 123).

The least common option for social structure involves independence of players, in which the success of one player or team is not related to the success of other players or teams. In *Rhythmical Red Light* (p. 102), partners moving from one line to the other line can be in charge of their own destiny. The scoring of one pair does not hinder or help another pair's scoring, as long as leaders utilize both a midline and endline for scoring. Although social contact between players may occur, socialization is incidental in that it is not critical to fulfill predetermined game goals.

The relationship between players in games receives a lot of attention due to peoples' desire to either promote or oppose traditional competition. Some proponents equate play and competition. Most proponents at least defend the status quo by claiming that competition is an unavoidable part of life, and that early game play provides a necessary foundation for experiencing competition in many situations later on. Parental support for this claim can be found in good measure (Walsh, 1987):

...it is a good idea to encourage children to participate in some form of physical activity whether it be a team or individual sport with some degree of competitiveness involved. Let's face it, today's world is competitive, and the better prepared our kids are for it, the better chance they have of being successful (p. 2).

Proponents further contend that competition provides the best means of being productive and having fun. Winning is viewed as the ultimate goal to achieve. Character development is thought to occur from players' responses to both winning and losing. Winning was given "top billing" at a 1993 Little League banquet. A retired professional baseball player gave the following advice to a room full of coaches:

We need to teach our players to win. That's the only way they walk away happy. When they lose they walk away with long faces and say, 'That umpire was awful', or 'Did you see how the other team cheated?' So they need to learn how to win.

The Little League speaker could have taken his cue from Vince Lombardi, one of the most heralded winners from the 1960's. To set the record straight, though, Lombardi did not say that winning is everything, as the misquotes often attest. Instead, he said that "Winning isn't everything; trying to win is" (Bavolek, 1993, p. 2; O'Brian, 1987, p. 197). The latter statement emphasizes striving to win, whereas the former idea requires actually winning to achieve success. Although Lombardi's correct quote is understandable in the professional ranks, neither the correct quote nor the misquote has any place in games with children and youth. More players can and will succeed if winning is a secondary goal, rather than a primary goal. Or, said another way, success in games for the masses depends on placing greater emphasis on the partnership model of competition than on the reward model of competition.

Those opposing competition for young children recognize that competing and cooperating are learned behaviors. Some claim that competition has detrimental effects on children's social behavior—that game structure encourages aggression and unfair play. Opponents are also concerned about the effects of competition on future participation due to children's demoralization (Ames, 1984; Robinson, 1989).

The single greatest concern of opponents is the effects of competition on self-esteem. Since traditional competition involves mutually exclusive goals, many players are destined to fail on a regular basis. Apparently, the Little League speaker overlooked inevitable failure. He did not mention that many of the young players could not achieve his goal. In a 20-game season, every team cannot mathematically win. Some teams win at the expense of others.

Ames (1984) reports that competitive environments tend to elevate the role of ability versus effort in players' thinking about their performance. The motivation of players of all abilities is cyclical. Those who perform well thrive in competitive environments and are likely to continue participating because they believe achievement depends on factors within their control. Consequently, failure is considered temporary and, therefore, does not reduce self-esteem. Players who do not perform well, however, believe that achievement depends on factors beyond their control. Failure is viewed more permanently, which in turn leads to lower self-esteem. Boys, in particular, use social comparisons to determine their standing among peers and corresponding self-esteem (Duda, 1981). Since self-esteem is closely linked to children's social comparisons, the relationship of social structure and other game elements to self-esteem is discussed in chapter 2.

Chapter 2

Game Elements and Self-esteem

Children and youth need key "building blocks" to develop self-esteem in a healthy way. This chapter addresses the building blocks, followed by an actual account of a child whose self-esteem was shaken for a time. The account will help game leaders consider the relationship between the elements of a game and self-esteem. The chapter concludes by suggesting ways to modify each game element so all players may be included.

Self-esteem Building Blocks

Self-esteem is learned. A child ascribes value to herself by seeing and hearing what others value in themselves, and by experiencing ways others react or treat her directly. Over time, images are gradually shaped and molded and given a sense of value or worth internally. Rainey and Rainey (1995) describe the images as a "composite":

Like a police department's composite sketch of a criminal suspect, [a child's] self-esteem is a composite drawing acquired from various sources and first hand accounts. But the drawing is not a black-and-white, one-dimensional, charcoal sketch. It is a full color, three-dimensional painting... (p. 21).

Building blocks contributing to self-esteem include worthiness, a sense of belonging, and competence. McDowell (1993) emphasizes that every person needs to build each block adequately to have a stable self-esteem. Stability might be measured by the degree to which people see themselves as God sees them—no more and no less.

Worthiness involves a person's acceptance of herself for who she is. In other words, people have inherent value. People's self-acceptance comes from understanding they are created in God's image (Genesis 1:27), given qualities according to His sovereign plan (Psalm 139:14) and personally atoned for by the blood of Christ (1 John 2:2). Leaders can show players they are worthy by treating them in a loving way even when those players do something wrong or fail to meet expectations (Romans 5:8).

A second building block to self-esteem involves a sense of **belonging**. In general, people sense they belong by recognizing their interconnectedness to others. People are designed to depend on one another for love (Romans 13:8), acceptance (Romans 15:7) and encouragement (1 Thessalonians 5:11). Interconnectedness in physical activities most often occurs when each person genuinely participates. Genuine participation requires more than group membership. It also requires that a player contribute to the group in a meaningful way. Genuine participation provides security because a person feels accepted by others. A prime example of insecurity stems from being chosen last for a team. Players chosen last may be tolerated by others, but not genuinely accepted. This underscores the importance of determining teams by methods that do not single players out, such as those described in chapter 8.

In addition to worthiness and a sense of belonging, people's **competence** or achievement lays a foundation for building self-esteem. Effects of competence on self-esteem are cyclical (Pangrazi, 1982): Successful experiences help people feel competent; competence enhances self-esteem; high self-esteem helps people take risks so they may experience continued success. Risk taking in this context refers to a player's emotional willingness to try something new, rather than to physical feats that may be dangerous.

Ideally, a player's self-esteem is not closely linked to competence, since God is primarily concerned with attitude (1 Samuel 16:7) and effort (Colossians 3:23). While this is the ideal to work toward, leaders need to recognize players' inconsistency in applying mature biblical principles. Even if young people are taught that self-esteem comes from God's love and acceptance, regardless of ability, most lack the spiritual and emotional maturity needed to overlook their inabilities and peer's reactions to them. Therefore, leaders need to monitor players' perceptions of failure so they view mistakes as learning opportunities, instead of as indicators of inferiority. Players need to understand that mistakes are normal and each person is gifted differently. Failing at tasks can motivate players to try other means of reaching goals. Players who fail to kick a ball hard on one occasion may approach the ball from a different angle or with different timing on the next try.

As leaders facilitate healthy attitudes toward failure, they also need to limit the amount of failure players experience. Failing at tasks can be motivating as long as a player's experiences are not characterized by failure overall (Dweck & Elliott, 1984). Overall failure is the unintended, if not the intended, message when leaders give elevated importance to succeeding at a particular task relative to other tasks, or when leaders design tasks so that failure occurs with inordinate frequency.

"Arranging the Blocks"

Play experiences of children and youth are recognized by teachers, parents and other leaders as a potential vehicle for enhancing character development. This explains, in part, why so many Christian education programs include recreational games as part of the curriculum (i.e. Christian schools, AWANA, Family Camp, Vacation Bible School). The complementary book to this work (Henkel, 2010) gives examples of ways to facilitate development of specific virtues in the context of game play.

Addressing the self-esteem aspect of character development during active games is particularly challenging, since the success and failure of young people is more open to scrutiny by peers than in other educational situations. For instance, someone's mistakes on a worksheet are often unnoticed by peers, whereas the one who finishes last in a relay is commonly ridiculed. Seeing active games through the eyes of a child may reveal unknown, deeply rooted feelings. Our oldest son's experience as a 5-year-old will be vivid in my mind for years to come. I still picture Brad participating unhappily in games at the neighborhood park — or was he genuinely participating?

Excluding Players

Brad entered a game of *Red Rover* on the first day of a summer playground program. At his request I watched from the side, and planned to slip away after activity had begun. Admittedly, I had well founded reservations about the recreational value of *Red Rover*, since the game involves only a few people at a time (Williams, 1994). 'But,' I thought, 'at least he'll enjoy being with the other children.' Two teams of 10 formed and stood in lines facing each other. Within Line B, arms were extended sideways with hands joined to prevent a member of Line A from running and breaking through. Then a player from Line B ran to attempt breaking through arms joined in Line A (and so on as the teams alternated turns). I watched child after child run to the other side and try to break through two outstretched joined arms—but not Brad. I watched child after child try to prevent others from running through their joined arms—but not Brad. 'Surely he'll get a turn,' I thought, 'It's just a matter of time'—but eventually time ran out.

My preconceived notions were confirmed. Brad actually stood there for nearly 20 minutes without having a turn or talking to anyone. I hurt inside, and I knew he did too. Oh yes, the children did complete crafts and other games after I left. Even so, I wondered if the initial game experience would have a lasting impact. When I returned to pick up Brad 90 minutes later, the answer was clear. His first remark was unsolicited: "I didn't get a turn in *Red Rover*." In other words, he felt excluded. He was somber and did not want to return to the program. My mind flashed back to the initial game, when I watched him fidget in line, with head down, waiting for his name to be called. (Refer to Figure 2.1.)

Red Rover, like many traditional competitive games, tends to exclude players. In other words, some children participate at the expense of others. Brad's self-esteem "checklist" drew a blank. Being excluded meant he didn't **belong**. He was unwanted. Being excluded meant no opportunity to show he was **competent**, even though he was. According to Dobson (2001), lack of opportunity to perform is often interpreted as lack of competence, because perceptions of physical ability can influence self-esteem to a greater extent than actual ability. Since Brad felt unwanted and incompetent, it was natural to feel **unworthy** also.

A week later before returning to the park, Brad asked with concern written all over his face: "Will they play *Red Rover* today"? Reassuring him he would have a good time, I asked one of the leaders to be sure he got a turn in whatever game was played. Unfortunately, a different leader took charge of games, and the same situation occurred again. Brad did not know many other children, and *Red Rover* depended on one group calling a member of the other group by name to "Come on over."

The purpose in describing Brad's experience is not to gain sympathy from others, nor is it to criticize recreation leaders. After all, even when program leaders have the best intentions, all players do not always get a turn during games. However, two important points may be underscored. First, Brad's experience is not an isolated case. During my experiences observing and leading physical activities in the church, camp and school settings, I have witnessed many instances of players being excluded.

Figure 2.1: Illustration of dejected player in *Red Rover*.

Second, situations like Brad's may be prevented by providing age appropriate games that include players. Brad's unfortunate experience was as much due to the elements of the game, as to the game leadership. Even when *Red Rover* is prolonged to give every person a chance, players are predominantly inactive, since each scoring attempt involves a single runner from one line, and two people with hands joined from the other line.

Including Players

The elements of a game need to remain flexible to include all players. Leaders who understand how to modify recreational games to accommodate different developmental levels can favorably influence the self-esteem of players. Entire books have addressed ways to modify games (Henkel, 1995; Morris & Stiehl, 1999). In this book and its complementary work (Henkel, 2010) a specific connection is made between game modification and character development. The next section of this book provides an overview of general principles for modifying game elements using the GAMES acronym. General principles are then applied through particular examples for the game *Red Rover*.

Goals

While not exhaustive, Table 2.1 highlights process and product goals for the game of *Baseball*. Process goals are measured while completing various tasks during a game, whereas product goals are measured by the outcome of a task or game overall. Goals are best modified by emphasizing the process of playing a game, and by emphasizing products of a game besides winning.

   Various goals in Table 2.1 correspond to different abilities of players. Players with limited ability should target primarily process goals. Process goals result from breaking down physical and social skills into specific achievable components. A player who seldom hits the ball can focus initially on assuming a good batting stance and swinging at strikes. Later the same player can concentrate on swinging down on the ball and making good contact. If a player focuses on particular components of skills, she may be satisfied with achieving a specific goal, regardless of the product of a task or game. Furthermore, the player can be fulfilled by giving maximum effort even when specific goals are not reached. Focusing on effort and specific achievements contributes to an unconditional self-esteem, because attention shifts away from the results of a player's performance.

Table 2.1

Suggested Process and Product Goals for Baseball *

BATTING	FIELDING FLY BALL
Assuming good stance	Getting jump on ball
Lining up knuckles on bat	Calling for ball
Swinging at strikes	Getting underneath ball
Stepping toward pitcher	Holding glove chin high
Swinging down on ball	Keeping elbows down
Actually making contact	Watching ball into glove
Following through with swing	Using two hands
Hitting fair ball	*Actually catching ball*
Hitting line drive	
Hitting sacrifice fly	

RUNNING BASES	THROWING BALL
Running hard on contact	Holding ball across seams
Running through first base	Stepping toward target
Rounding bases	Straightening arm initially
Running on every force out	Pointing thumb down
Running with two outs	Following through with
Tagging up on fly ball	step
Safely reaching base	*Throwing to correct base*
Stealing base	*Throwing ball accurately*
Scoring run	*Throwing runner out*

FIELDING GROUND BALL	BEING SPORTSMANLIKE
Assuming proper position in field	Respecting position assignments
Assuming proper stance	Exhibiting self-control following error
Charging ball	Accepting umpire's call
Getting in front of ball	Consoling teammate
Keeping glove on ground	Complimenting opponent
Knocking ball down	*Shaking opponent's hand*
Fielding ball cleanly	

* Italicized items indicate product goals.

Product goals are italicized in Table 2.1, and represent game outcomes, such as the culmination of performing a skill or applying strategy. Players with greater ability may pursue product goals along with process goals. Those who regularly make contact with the bat could focus on hitting fair balls, and then line drives. Strategy may involve trying to hit a sacrifice fly or trying to hit to the opposite field. Players need to be careful to limit emphasis placed on product goals, since product goals depend on the performance of other players to a greater degree than process goals. A player's success in hitting a line drive depends on where and how hard the opposing pitcher throws the ball. A player's success in throwing out an opponent depends on the opponent's speed, and on a teammate's ability to be at the appropriate base and catch the ball.

Alignment

The alignment of a game includes players by giving them equal opportunity to be involved. Equal opportunity requires having equal access to equipment. In some alignments, such as a circle or square, players have equal access as long as leaders prevent assertive players from dominating. Domination occurs when one player intentionally or unintentionally steps in front of others to make plays.

Alignments for some games tend to include players at certain positions more than others. In *Baseball*, players generally consider the outfield (particularly right field) undesirable because few balls are hit that far. In *Soccer*, defensive positions are less desirable than offensive positions because players like to score. In *Football*, less gifted players are often relegated to the role of a blocker play after play.

Alignments can be changed to place various positions on equal par with one other. In *Square Soccer* (p. 101), for instance, all players simultaneously serve on offense and defense. When a ball comes to players they try to prevent it from crossing their lines, then try to kick it across one of the opponent's two lines (other two sides of the square). When field positions cannot be arranged on equal par, players can rotate through positions in an organized manner to allow all individuals to play more varied and desirable roles. Rotating positions does not necessarily mean that all players should play all positions. Every person does not have the ability to play pitcher or quarterback. Placing a player in a position where he walks batters around the bases may do more harm emotionally than limiting his participation to less "desirable" roles.

Movements

Player success performing movements in games depends on both quantity and quality of practice opportunities. Quantity of practice refers to how often a skill is repeated. To achieve an optimum number of skill repetitions players need to first practice skills in isolation from games. By working alone or in pairs players are able to increase consistency, without regard to strategy and other team concepts.

Once people achieve basic competency in skills, repetition is enhanced by playing games with small numbers and/or by providing enough equipment. This is one reason Werner (1989) recommends that children play net/wall type activities before other games. By contrast, players engaged in a traditional *Kickball* game may only kick the ball twice, and throw the ball once—or not at all (Wilson, 1976). Instead of the common practice of playing one game with 20 to 30 people, leaders are encouraged to organize two games with 10 to 15 people. In addition, leaders might consider having two pitchers and two kickers at a time. The two kickers could run opposite directions around the bases, as in *Double Trouble* (p. 133). This format requires more adult guidance, a small price to pay to provide enough repetition of skills.

Quality of practice refers to how well a skill is performed. Skill quality is enhanced by providing a relaxed, nonthreatening practice environment, by giving specific feedback about performance, and/or by breaking skills down into basic forms. A relaxed environment allows players to practice skills at their pace "out of the spotlight." Although *Dribble Tag* (p. 125) is not relaxed because opponents try to knock away other balls, an individual player can determine the level of stress experienced by standing near the center of activity or on the periphery. The game keeps players out of the spotlight by requiring enough concentration to maintain control of one's ball, that watching others perform is very difficult. The game also tends to foster good quality skill because dribbling a ball too high, or otherwise out of control, makes it easier to knock away. In contrast to *Dribble Tag*, relays are often threatening to children because so much emphasis is placed on speed and those finishing last are in the spotlight. Due to the stress and lack of opportunity experienced by young people in many relays (Schwager, 1992; Williams, 1992), chapter 7 gives specific ideas for helping relays be viable educational experiences.

Feedback about performance influences quality of practice by telling performers what to focus on. Leaders are encouraged to balance general supportive comments with specific information about a skill. So, a leader could compliment a player on an overhand throw by saying, "Nice job stepping with the opposite foot," rather than just saying, "Nice throw."

Leaders are also encouraged to use specific supportive comments prior to corrective comments. For instance, a leader could say, "I like the way you called for the ball. Next time try to get underneath it a little further."

A third way to enhance quality of practice is by simplifying skills, or breaking them down into basic forms. Batting in *T-ball*, for instance, allows players to hit a stationary ball off a tee. Although more players are successful hitting a stationary ball, higher skilled youngsters may lose interest from not being challenged. This is a drawback of tailoring movements to the lower skilled players only.

In addition to modifying a movement in the same way for all players, leaders may allow players to choose from among movement alternatives. This provides the best challenge for all players, since children of the same chronological age normally span three to four years developmentally. In *Kickball*, for example, players could choose between kicking a rolling ball from the pitcher, or a stationary ball resting at home plate. The alternative allows less advanced players to perform the easier task of kicking a still object. Since players tend to choose options that provide success, they potentially feel more competent. Over time, the sense of competence contributes to the development of self-esteem.

Equipment

Choices for game equipment are many and varied. Common characteristics of equipment include the size, shape and amount. Size of equipment needs to correspond to the size of players' hands and/or feet. An overhand throw requires a small enough ball so a player can grip it well. Conversely, catching requires a large enough ball so a player can visually track it well.

The shape of equipment is also crucial to success. Players have an easier time catching a round playground ball than a football. Yet, when throwing a large object overhand, the football shape provides a better grip than a playground ball.

The amount of equipment in a game dramatically influences a player's level of participation. The more people in a game, the more necessary it is to add equipment. Adding equipment gives opportunities to perform skills to players who would not otherwise have a chance. In some cases, a game may allow each player to have a balloon or ball, as in *Raindrops* (p. 103) or *Dribble Tag* (p. 125), respectively. In other cases, however, equipment needs to be limited, even in large group games. Limiting equipment helps insure safety and facilitates players' social relationships. In a game such as *Frisbee Frame* (p. 135), players would spend most of their time dodging and chasing discs if more than two per team were included.

Social structure

As with enhancing skill practice, leaders can effectively modify the social structure of games by limiting the number of players per game. Organizing two games with 10 to 15 players offers twice the participation as one game with 20 to 30 players. When a game is being taught for the first time, leaders may begin with one large game and form two games after rules are understood. Once players are in smaller groups, leaders can more effectively monitor taking of turns.

In addition to having smaller groups, social structure can be changed by the way in which players relate to one another. In most traditional games, players try to beat each other. Since success depends largely on winning, many players are left with a feeling of failure. Players who focus on the outcome of winning hold this as a condition for accepting themselves. Indeed, Kohn (1992) describes competition as more of a psychological need than a desire: "We compete to overcome fundamental doubts about our capabilities and, finally, to compensate for low self-esteem (p. 99)." Even the skillful performer is not insured of high self-esteem according to Walker (1980), since the recognition that victory brings is temporary:

> *Winning doesn't satisfy us—we need to do it again, and again. The taste of success seems merely to whet the appetite for more. When we lose, the compulsion to seek future success is overpowering; the need to get [in the game] the following weekend is irresistible. We cannot quit when we are ahead or after we've won, and we certainly cannot quit when we're behind or after we've lost. We are addicted* (p. 37).

By providing young people with experiences in games involving competitive, cooperative and independent social structures, the impact of a particular social structure or game is more balanced. In order to apply the principles for modifying game elements, the following section provides three formats for modifying the game *Red Rover*. Game leaders are encouraged to evaluate formats based on the goals they wish to accomplish.

Formats for Modifying *Red Rover*

Game 1

Figure 2.2 illustrates three different formats for modifying the game *Red*

Rover. In Game 1, the social structure is modified to limit the number of players to 10, rather than 20, per game. Players probably wouldn't be overlooked on a team of only 5 people. Even so, the game requires additional modifications so that more than 6 players can be involved at a time (indicated by darkened players).

Game 2

A second format for modifying *Red Rover* limits number of players and provides for a range of ability levels. Game 2 allows all players to be appropriately challenged by choosing from alternatives provided. Players choose who to tag, and how many times to tag opponents. On signal, Lines B and D dodge about freely (change in movement) within the boundaries without letting hands come apart (change in social structure). Runners from Lines A and C try to tag either end player from Lines B and D, respectively, and return "home" as quickly as possible (change in goal). Home is represented by the player's original place in line. The same taggers repeat this procedure as often as they choose in a minute, scoring one point each time they tag either end player. Naturally, runners from Lines A and C alternate with those from Lines B and D, while players in Lines A and C join hands. People also take turns as end players of their respective lines (rotating alignment).

For additional challenge, runners could be required to forfeit all points scored for not returning home before the minute lapses. The additional rule would dramatize each runner's choice to risk or not risk multiple tagging attempts. In Game 2, 12 people are actively involved during each scoring attempt, since players are divided into four teams, and two teams move throughout the playing area at a time. Active involvement provides a greater sense of belonging, one of the building blocks to self-esteem.

Game 3

A third format for modifying *Red Rover* involves change for all game elements, and provides more participation than Games 1 or 2. Game 3 provides a common goal for all but the tagger (change in social structure). On signal, all players join hands and dodge about freely (change in movement) in their respective lines. One designated tagger tries to tag as many end players as possible in a minute, returning "home" following each tag (change in goal). Home is represented by a centrally located circle or hoop (change in equipment). Players' performances are enhanced by each other as they all try to move cooperatively in their

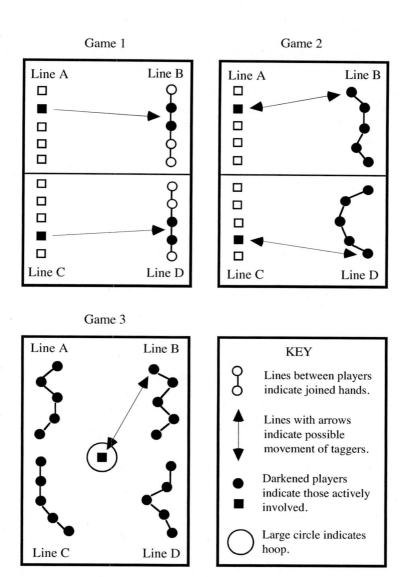

Figure 2.2: Illustration of different formats for modifying the game *Red Rover*.

respective lines with hands joined. As in Game 2, people take turns as end players of their respective lines (rotating alignment). In addition to having a common goal, players in Game 3 are as active as possible, with all players involved during each scoring attempt. (See *Chain Tag*, p. 123, for a more extensive explanation.)

The three formats for modifying *Red Rover* might suggest that game alternatives should necessarily result in a cooperative social structure. However, chapter 3 emphasizes that both cooperative and competitive games can provide worthwhile learning experiences for players in a way that enhances self-esteem. The myth of needing to choose between competition *or* cooperation is exposed, before suggesting ways to monitor people's competitiveness.

Chapter 3

Competition *and* Cooperation

Many programs involving games for children and youth are based upon common assumptions regarding the benefits of traditional competition. Each assumption is examined here before giving evidence for the value of cooperative games. Then guidelines are given for monitoring competition so players may successfully participate in recreational experiences with any social structure.

Assumptions About Competition

The first assumption about the benefits of competition might be called **preparation**, that is, games in which players try to beat each other prepare them to cope with the competitive "daily grind" experienced throughout life. Those who hold to this assumption claim that competition is part of human nature. While the claim is unsubstantiated, people may conclude competitive behavior is inevitable, believing it is more readily observable than cooperative behavior. At the same time, many experts believe competition is learned rather than inevitable, as reflected by Tutko and Bruns (1976):

Competition is a learned phenomenon...people are not born with a motivation to win or to be competitive. We inherit a potential for a degree of activity, and we all have the instinct to survive. But the will to win comes through training and the influences of one's family and environment (p. 53).

Those who believe competition is learned also point out that providing players with opportunities to cooperate in game experiences would more accurately reflect life's daily challenges than requiring them to compete (Grineski, 1996).

A second presumed benefit of competition could be called **production**. Proponents of competition believe that trying to beat others results in the greatest productivity and achievement. Ironically, conclusive evidence demonstrates that cooperation, rather than competition, promotes high achievement and productivity. Johnson and Maruyama et al. (1981) reviewed 122 studies from 1924 to 1980 that compared achievement within competitive, cooperative and independent social structures. Results indicated that in 65 studies cooperation promoted higher achievement than competition, whereas only 8 studies found the reverse effect. Cooperation resulted in higher achievement than an independent social structure in 108 studies, whereas only 6 studies found the opposite. Cooperation was reported as the most advantageous social structure regardless of the subject area or age group.

Participation may be considered a third presumed benefit of competition. It is widely believed that children prefer to participate in competitive activities more than in alternative activities. This misconception stems largely from the fact that adults socialize children to compete, and to want to compete (Kohn, 1992). Orlick (1978) found the reverse to be true among third, fourth and fifth graders: "Given the choice, two thirds of the nine and ten year old boys and all of the girls would prefer to play games where neither side loses rather than games where one side wins and the other side loses" (p. 177). Children gave many reasons for preferring games with no losers, including: "It's more fun when everyone is working together," "You won't feel so bad 'cause you lost," and "I usually get a turn" (p. 178).

A fourth assumption about competition's benefits concerns **purification**. Proponents have long claimed that participating in sports enhances moral development and the building of character. Moral development is often measured by analyzing player's reasoning about moral issues. Unfortunately, studies have found that moral reasoning is less mature when referenced to a sport specific setting than to a nonsport setting (Bredemeier & Shields, 1984, 1986). The reverse effect would be expected if sports participation enhances moral development. One of the problems in supporting claims that participating in sports builds character, is in defining and measuring character. Attempts to examine specific behaviors, such as sharing and honesty, are inconclusive for competitive settings. By contrast, Orlick (1981) found that preschool children exposed to cooperative games for several months shared more with their peers when given the choice of keeping candy for themselves or giving it away.

As with the other assumptions, the building of character in sport settings is not an inevitable result. Consequently, discussion in the companion book (Henkel, 2010) provides ways to be more intentional about accomplishing this priority. The remainder of this chapter continues to contrast competitive and cooperative experiences, and addresses ways to monitor competition so whatever social structure players experience, they may benefit from recreational play.

Some people question whether cooperative activities are as challenging as competitive activities, since challenge within sports is often presumed to be synonymous with trying to beat others. Those holding this view may have limited experience with cooperative activities. Authors on cooperative games offer very challenging activities, some which have been available for half a century. Lentz and Cornelius (1950) suggest *Cooperative Bowling*, which involves knocking down the pins in as many rounds as there are players. Orlick (1982) recommends a *Group Obstacle Course* in which players overcome each obstacle without releasing their joined hands. Midura and Glover (1995, 1992) describe more than 30 activities organized by different degrees of challenge.

Claiming that either cooperative or competitive games offer more challenge is an oversimplified argument. After all, one can find examples of both types of games with very limited challenge. Instead of claiming superiority with regard to challenge, one could think of cooperative and competitive games as simply posing different kinds of challenges (Henkel, 1997, 1995). Therefore, by engaging in both types of games (and independent games), players get a greater variety of experiences.

Although similar benefits may be found in games of all social structures to different degrees, benefits of traditional competitive and independent games are often offset by disadvantages. Competitive games tend to produce stress and anxiety more reflective of the American work ethic than of a leisure time pursuit. Stress is one of the reasons cited for why about 75% of youth drop out of organized sports programs (Bavolek, 1993; Orlick, 1978). Granted, competitive games within school or church curricula may be less intense than in organized sports programs. Yet, enough intensity can exist to counter much of the fun experienced. Although independent games are less stressful than competitive games, social goals are seldom realized, since the fun obtained through social contact is more incidental than planned.

Extremists opposing competition believe the problem is competition itself (Kohn, 1992), rather than the social context in which it occurs (Gould, 1984). While the concerns of competition opponents are warranted, the concerns do not require choosing between cooperation *or* competition for players eight years and older. People can cooperate *and* compete under the proper guidance. Although convincing evidence refutes common assumptions of win-based competition, nonwin-based competition can result in positive ends when quality leadership is present (Coakley, 1990; Martens, 1978). Certainly my experiences teaching and coaching for 30 years support the opinion that competitive games can result in constructive ends when game leaders and participants consciously monitor the way they compete, and the extent of their competitiveness.

Monitoring the Way We Compete

Monitoring the way we compete requires distinguishing between a competitive situation and competitive attitude. Kohn (1992) refers to these constructs as "structural competition" and "intentional competition," respectively (p. 3), and they are key in helping balance the reward and partnership models of competition. Monitoring the way we compete requires awareness of our intentional competition in a structurally competitive situation. In other words, once the choice is made to compete with a game structure that embodies a reward model, how can teachers, coaches and other leaders help players display healthy attitudes and behaviors characteristic of a partnership model? I maintain, as does Kohn, that one can have structural competition without intentional competition, and vice versa. In most situations, however, the amount of structural and intentional competition might be most accurately considered on a continuum, rather than claiming competition does or does not exist.

Hypothetical continuums for structural and intentional competition are superimposed in Figure 3.1. (Henkel, 1997, 1995). The figure could be helpful in monitoring how competitive a particular game experience is. Location of points on the continuum are relative to one another, not absolute. Even though points represent different contexts for the sport of *Baseball*, principles could apply to any physical activity setting.

Professional baseball players operate within a highly competitive context structurally, given their drafting procedures, multimillion-dollar contracts, and demanding schedules. Most players are rather high in intentional competition as well (upper right corner in Figure 3.1), since maintaining a roster spot depends on performance and the ultimate goal is to reach the World Series.

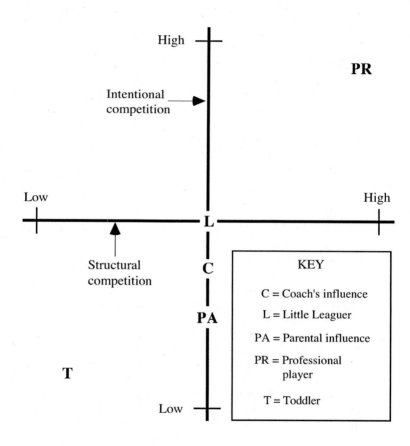

Figure 3.1: Hypothetical relative amounts of structural and intentional competition in *Baseball*.

One could place an Instructional Little League experience somewhere near the middle of the continuum (Point L in Figure 3.1). Although the league is structurally competitive, the rules promote less structural competition than found in professional sports, as expected. Game modifications are adapted to the particular age group, but are inflexible once play begins. The modifications change, to a degree, the way players compete. For example, the league requires that all players participate in at least four innings, including one in the infield, and one in the outfield. All players bat in a regular rotation, regardless whether or not they are assigned a position in the field that inning. Stealing second and third base is permitted provided the pitch has crossed home plate. In addition, no scores or league standings are emphasized.

As with professional athletes, players on a Little League team actually develop different levels of intentional competition, largely based on the influence of the coach and parents. Our boy's coach, for instance, took several steps to reduce or downplay the level of intentional competition (Point C in Figure 3.1). First of all, he emphasized three goals at the beginning of the season, none of which included winning games:

1. Have fun.
2. Improve skills.
3. Make new friends.

Interestingly, the goals correspond to the top three goals ranked by children who participate in athletics (Gould, 1984). The goals of our boy's coach were put in writing to parents, spoken to players at the initial organizational meeting, and reinforced several times throughout the season. The goals are just as appropriate for school, church and other community settings. Additional goals could address aspects of character development at the discretion of leaders.

To help fulfill the goals, the coach rotated all players but the pitcher to positions every inning (more frequently than the league required) and did not emphasize the score during or after the game. Rotating players helped them work on the broadest range of skills, even though fewer runs would have scored against the team with stronger players in key positions. Although some players knew the score without the coach's help, not talking about it still made a statement, particularly since the coach willingly bypassed opportunities to score runs. He preferred to hold a runner at third base for the next batter to hit in, rather than having the runner take advantage of sloppy fielding by the other team. Lack of attention to the score was also regularly evident in many youth soccer games I coached, as evidenced by some players not knowing the outcome at the end of games.

Weissinger (1994) claims a teacher or coach cannot "have his cake and eat it too," meaning a leader cannot promote competitive games, yet minimize scoring. Since learners in physical education regard scoring as the main criteria for succeeding in a game, Weissinger believes leaders need to either (a) accept the importance of scoring to players and, thereby increase scoring opportunities, or (b) reject the importance of scoring and try to change players' emphasis on it. The reason the choices are dichotomous is that our society associates scoring too closely with winning. In fact, winning the contest is often so central to success that many athletes and spectators have difficulty accepting a close loss. If their team cannot win, some people would rather "lose big" than face the disappointment of almost winning. Such a view disregards other viable reasons for scoring. Weissinger (1994) found that children's reasons for scoring in physical education were more tied to personal accomplishment, than to beating the opponent, as conveyed by the following specific statements: "I made a home run in *Kickball*," "I made the most goals in *Hockey*," and "I got the flag back when we were playing *Capture the Flag*" (p. 432).

Leaders have at least one more choice in addition to those offered by Weissinger. Like our boy's Little League coach, leaders can accept player's need to score, yet reject the importance of scoring for the sake of winning. Scoring is an important culminating activity. When people play hard individually and collectively, scoring provides a sense of accomplishment. In contrast, I once watched a youth basketball game in which one team trailed 20-0 at halftime. I would not want my child to be in that scoreless situation—not because scoring helps a team win—but because scoring is a way to measure the success of performing skills and working together. This isn't to say that performing skills and working together cannot be appreciated unless scoring occurs. Our son Craig, for instance, once remarked, "I think I played my best soccer game" following a 2-1 loss, in which he did not score. Even though he scored multiple goals in several other games, he was able to focus on alternative goals (examples for Little League suggested in Table 2.1). In Craig's case, he based his success partly on having twice just missed the net after contacting two corner kicks with his head. Much of the motivation for playing games is found in the various challenges provided. Getting a base hit is one challenge; sacrifice bunting a player to second base is a different challenge; actually driving the runner home presents yet another challenge. With or without winning, the challenge of scoring provides a different sense of accomplishment than the other challenges. When possible, redefining what constitutes a score helps more players feel accomplished. In Little League baseball, means of scoring is predetermined. In less structured physical activity settings, however, leaders have an opportunity to modify scoring. For instance, when modifying *Kickball,* children could score one point for each base reached.

Parents, as well as coaches, may influence players' levels of intentional competition. Parental influence may be largely determined by the degree to which they reinforce the coach's goals, and by additional goals parents have (Point PA in Figure 3.1). In our case, we reinforced the coach's goals before, during, and after each game in some way. Occasionally, when our team was batting, I would walk over by the bench and say, "Who's having fun"? just to make sure that goal did not get lost in the intensity of the game. When another parent could be heard saying, "Hit a home run," I would be yelling, "Just good contact, now" to encourage the player to focus on an immediate aspect of the skill, rather than the outcome.

Additional goals we emphasized as parents were to appreciate opponents and to respect the umpire. I modeled appreciation for opponents by complimenting them for extraordinary effort or performance. When several players from our team criticized the umpire following a game, I suggested that the coach stress the following principles at the next practice:

1. Umpires are human and will make mistakes like anyone else.
2. We need to respect umpire's calls even when we disagree.
3. Calls of the umpire seldom determine the outcome of a game. Generally mistaken calls even out for both teams.

Our boy definitely "bought in" to the Little League goals. About one week into the season, without prompting, he prayed that God would help him achieve the goals—spoken word for word as the coach said them. At season's end he prayed again, thanking God that he actually achieved the goals. His positive attitude throughout the season (albeit not every minute) was particularly encouraging, given that his team finished with a "losing" record. Whether leaders supported the Little League program or the specific coaching techniques described, the broader principle to underscore is that players were successful in focusing on the process of playing the game, and on products of the game besides winning.

Monitoring the Extent of Our Competitiveness

If the way people compete refers to attitudes and conduct in a setting that calls for competition structurally, then the extent of a person's competitiveness refers to (a) her level of intentional competition when structural competition is low, and (b) when she chooses to enter a structurally competitive setting.

The extent of a toddler's competitiveness is largely determined by parental decisions. Our son Trent's experience as a toddler batting in the back yard is depicted in Figure 3.1 at the opposite end of the continuum from the professional athlete (bottom left corner). Structurally, he had no opponent because his goal was simply to make contact. Granted, Trent was more satisfied when he hit the ball forward than backward. In addition, he sometimes dropped the bat and ran in a circle following a "hit," but he clearly was not trying to beat anybody. As long as I maintained a relaxed posture without undue expectations of him, Trent's experience was basically noncompetitive. If, however, I would have compared his performance with his older brother's performance, the extent of my competitiveness would increase and Trent's experience would shift to the right in the figure.

The extent of one's competitiveness is also determined by when the person chooses to compete in a structurally competitive setting. When a person competes is reflected by the age of onset and the frequency of participating thereafter. Parents again contribute to a player's competitiveness (or lack thereof) through decisions made on the player's behalf. Parents who enter a child into organized sports at the earliest possible age increase the extent of a child's competitiveness. Leaders in some school and community sport programs have discretion to help parents make wise choices by delaying the onset of competitive games. Many college students of mine have told me their dislike for physical activity began in the primary grades as a result of failure in competitive games. Baumgarten (1988) addressed this concern with his plea to avoid regular competition in school settings until age 10:

> *There is absolutely no need to spread the evils of competition among our five [to] nine-year-olds in school settings through a steady diet of Dodgeball, Kickball, Relay Races, and other mass games, which, by their very nature, prevent so many children from feeling good about themselves and their movement abilities, and which are usually detrimental to the development and improvement of motor skills* (p. 38).

Midura and Glover (1999) reinforced Baumgarten's guideline by recommending that school curricula up through third grade focus on a play-oriented approach that fosters development of motor skills.

Leaders and parents, of course, recognize that players of the same age may differ considerably in developmental level. Therefore, no "magic age" for beginning competition exists. At the same time, not many children possess the physical skills or emotional maturity to compete at ages five or six. Consequently, our sons skipped *T-ball* and began Little League *Baseball* at age eight after they expressed interest.

After competition is eventually introduced to children, the extent of their competitiveness can be monitored by controlling how often competitive games are played. A first grader may benefit most by experiencing only cooperative and independent games. A fourth grader might participate in a balance of cooperative, competitive and independent games. A seventh grader can handle more competitive games, but would still benefit from experiencing some degree of balance.

The exact balance between games of different social structures is not the issue. The critical things to monitor are the values being promoted in recreational games—whatever the social structure—and to what degree players internalize those values. The games outlined in Part II promote healthy values and character development. By internalizing values, players can keep their competitiveness in perspective. Providing games in which all players genuinely participate and feel good about their experience is a good place to start. To address character development in a more direct way consult the companion book, *Integrating Active Games with Other Subjects* (Henkel, 2010).

Part II

Game Choices in Process

Part II provides leaders with 94 games to use in a variety of educational settings as an integral part of their larger purposes. The number of games is intentionally limited to emphasize variety and uniqueness of games, rather than sheer numbers.

Games in Part II are outlined using a "3-D" format. A **description** of each game provides information for elements discussed in chapter 1. **Directions** for each game provide leaders with a suggested sequence for explaining rules and possible alternatives. Where helpful, game outlines also include a **diagram** that clarifies boundaries and player positioning.

In classifying games, authors have accounted for the skills involved (i.e. sending an object away [Mauldon & Redfern, 1981]), the object of a game (i.e. scoring runs [Thorpe & Bunker, 1986]), and the type of cooperation required (i.e. collective scoring [Orlick, 1978]). Games in chapters 4 through 6 are organized by the number of players involved, because the variety of games represented does not "fit" well into other classification schemes. In addition, the size of a given group is a significant factor in selecting a game. Of course, a large group may be divided into smaller groups of any size or into pairings to accommodate a game. Chapter 4 contains 15 active game ideas for partners. A collection of 32 small group games is provided in chapter 5. An additional 30 large group games are the focus of chapter 6.

Games in chapter 7 apply to a variety of group sizes. Instead of organizing activities by group size, chapter 7 specifically targets 17 relay games to underscore their viability as a worthwhile game form. Common criticisms of relays are both exposed and alleviated.

Chapter 8 deals with game administration. Once a leader chooses an appropriate game, the leader needs to provide an environment conducive to realizing the game's goals. Administrative aspects discussed here include pregame responsibilities, such as determining teams and explaining procedures, and actual game responsibilities, such as monitoring time and encouraging players.

Games in Part II strike a balance between competitive and cooperative activities, along with a few independent games. Leaders are reminded that game elements must remain flexible. The choices are always "in process." A particular game may work with one group, yet need to be modified or even eliminated with another. Leaders need to carefully observe players and monitor to what degree all are genuinely participating. More than that, leaders can monitor to what degree all players learn something and feel good about their effort in meeting a challenge, for this is the true measure of a game's success.

Games in each chapter are sequenced by the recommended ages of participants. A range is provided for each game, beginning as young as age five and extending as old as age 14 and up. An index lists games by chapter in the order presented (see p. 177). The index also indicates the national standards for physical education best addressed by each activity (see p. 180). The national standards correspond to important outcomes for physical activity identified by the National Association for Sport and Physical Education (NASPE, 2004). Note that while the index highlights Standards 1, 2, 4, and 5, Standards 3 and 6 may be addressed by most any game, depending on the emphasis and dialogue provided by leaders.

Chapter 4

Games for Partners

G ames for partners are simple in alignment, since only two people are involved. Although players typically face each other at close range, this alignment becomes more complex when players are required to move back and forth, as in *Butterfly Four Square* (p. 45). Many body parts and movements may be incorporated into a game for two, but a limited number are normally used at any given time. This trend is not universal, however, as reflected in the game *Busy Bodies* (p. 38) in which players use as many different body parts as possible. As with movements, game equipment may be varied across games for two, but probably limited within a given game.

Regardless which social structure is utilized, players normally interact in simple terms as well. Whether a game is competitive or cooperative, focusing on only one other player is considerably easier than monitoring the play of several others simultaneously. Due to the simple nature of games for partners, many are well suited for primary school age children. For games with a choice of social structure, the competitive version is intended for children near the older end of the recommended range.

(1) BUSY BODIES

Description

Goals: Improve body awareness.
                Understand strategies for using many body parts.
                Practice striking.

Alignment: Partners standing facing each other.

Movements: Striking.

Equipment: One 10- to 12-inch balloon for every two people.

Social   Competitive or cooperative.
   structure: 2 players, ages 5 to 9.

Directions

Instruct players to alternate striking the balloon back and forth, with upward or sideward trajectory. Require each successive hit to be made with a different body part. Encourage players to call out each body part used since some body parts are difficult to distinguish (i.e. finger, hand, wrist). Once a mistake is made in a given round, players may use the same body part(s) again during ensuing rounds.

In the cooperative version (any age), have players count the total number of hits made before the balloon hits the floor. In the competitive version (ages 7-9), have players try to be the last one to strike the balloon while naming a body part. Do not have players intentionally try to strike the balloon toward the floor or keep it from the opponent.

Alternative: For additional challenge, require children to play the game while balancing on just one foot (allowing movement on that foot).

(2) FIST LIST

Description

Goals: Name information according to categories.
Understand strategies for listing multiple ideas.
Use striking skills in game situation.

Alignment: Standing facing a partner.

Movements: Balancing, striking one-handed.

Equipment: One 10- to 12-inch balloon for every two people.

Social
structure: Competitive or cooperative.
2 players, ages 5 to 10.

Directions

Instruct players to alternate striking the balloon back and forth using their fists with some upward or sideward trajectory. As each hit is made, tell the respective player to list (by calling out) another name of an item from a designated category, without repeating a name. For instance, if the category is desserts players could call out "cake," "pie," "cookie," etc. until no more can be named. Select categories based on the player's developmental levels. Younger children may enjoy naming colors or farm animals. Older children could name states or occupations.

After children have played a couple rounds, have them strike the balloon with an open hand or heel of the hand, instead of their fists. Emphasize the advantage of these techniques due to the larger surface area (open hand) or contour (heel of hand) that contacts the balloon. In the competitive version (ages 7-10) have each player try to be the last one to strike the balloon and name an item. In the cooperative version (any age) have players count the total number of items named, assuming the balloon was hit each time. Do not have players intentionally try to strike the balloon toward the floor or keep it from the opponent.

Alternative: For additional challenge, require children to play the game while balancing on just one foot (allowing movement on that foot).

(3) BALLOON KEEP AWAY

Description

Goals: Improve body awareness.
             Understand and practice guarding and striking.

Alignment: Standing facing partner, scattered throughout playing
             area.

Movements: Guarding, striking one- or two-handed.

Equipment: One 10- to 12-inch balloon for every two people.

Social   Competitive.
  structure: 2 players, ages 7 to 11.

Directions

Instruct Player X to begin striking the balloon in the air and guarding it
from Player Y. Tell Player Y to intercept the balloon and get control by
holding it with two hands. Award Player Y one point each time he gets
control of the balloon. Give Player Y an additional point each time
Player X commits one of the following errors:

1. Letting balloon touch the floor
2. Letting balloon get above head height
3. Trapping balloon in hands or against body.

Do not give Player Y a point if he causes the balloon to hit the floor or go
above head height. Each time Player Y gets the balloon, have him return
it to Player X to initiate activity again within a 30-second time frame. If
Player X controls the balloon for 30 seconds without error Player Y
scores no points. When time expires have players reverse roles for the
next round. A game consists of six 30-second rounds, with players
alternating who begins with the balloon.

Alternative: For additional challenge, increase length of rounds to 60
seconds.

(4) HALF COURT

Description

Goals: Practice striking in game situation.
Improve hand-eye coordination.

Alignment: Standing behind the service line on tennis or pickleball courts with four players per court.

Movements: Throwing and catching.

Equipment: One playground or gator ball per pair, four polydots or strips of tape.

Social
   structure: Competitive.
2 players, ages 7 to 12.

Directions

Place hash marks with tape or polydots half way between the net and service line on each half court. Determine partners and have them stand across from each other behind their respective service lines. Instruct players to alternate throwing the ball into the opposite service box (straight across, not diagonally) to prevent the opponent from catching it on a fly or on one bounce. Each successful throw scores one point. Each throw that lands out of bounds subtracts one point. Lines are considered in bounds as in any net game. Players may go anywhere to catch the ball, but must throw it from behind a hash mark half way between the net and service line. Rotate partners every three minutes and have players keep their running scores.

Alternative: If throwers are too successful, require two-handed throws.

(5) FAB GRAB

Description

Goals: Practice starting and stopping in game situation.
              Understand possible outcomes of taking a risk.
              Improve reaction time.

Alignment: Standing facing partner 30 feet away.

Movements: Grabbing, running, tagging.

Equipment: One beanbag per couple, cones to mark lines.

Social   Competitive.
  structure: 2 players, ages 7 to 12.

Directions

Divide players in two groups and have them stand in lines 30 feet across from their corresponding partners. Place one beanbag on the floor midway between each set of partners. On signal, instruct players to run to the middle near their beanbag. Have players try to score in one of two ways:

1. Grabbing the beanbag and returning to the initial line without being tagged scores 2 points (i.e. *Fab Grab* [fabulous grab]).

2. Tagging the opponent before she returns to her line with the beanbag scores 1 point.

Rotate partners after every two rounds and have players keep their running scores.

Alternative: For variety, place the beanbags on the top of cones, instead of on the floor.

(6) TIMELY BOUNCE

Description

Goals: Improve hand-eye coordination.
Understand possible outcomes of risking more bounces.
Improve reaction time.

Alignment: Standing facing partner three steps apart.

Movements: Bouncing, catching.

Equipment: One reaction ball for every two players, one polydot for every player.

Social structure: Competitive.
2 players, ages 7 to 12.

Directions

Instruct players to stand on their polydots three steps apart and face each other. Have Partner X begin play by dropping the ball while holding it head high. Instruct Player Y to catch the ball after a select number of bounces; the more bounces, the more risk:

1 bounce = 1 point
2 bounces = 2 points
3 bounces = 3 points, and so on

When the ball begins rolling or is otherwise out of control no points can be earned. Have partners change roles following each turn. Players try to be the first to reach 21 points exactly. If 21 points is exceeded have players count backward and forward again if necessary (i.e. a player with 20 points who accidentally catches the ball after two bounces, temporarily reverts back to 18 points).

Alternative: For additional challenge, have players drop the ball from waist high and/or move dots one step further apart.

(7) REACTION BALL

Description

Goals: Practice reacting quickly.
                    Practice blocking.
                    Practice kicking accurately.

Alignment: One player standing near goal; other player facing goal
                    20 feet away.

Movements: Catching, kicking.

Equipment: Nerf soccer ball, markers to designate one goal.

Social   Competitive.
   structure: 2 players, ages 7 to 12.

Directions

Instruct Players X and Y to stand facing the goal, as indicated by the arrows in Diagram 4.1. Have Player Y yell "kick," as a signal for Player X to kick the ball at the goal below the waist. Do not allow balls kicked above the waist to be re-kicked. Instruct Player Y to turn around quickly and try to block the ball from entering the goal area. Follow the same procedure two more times from 15 and 10 feet away, respectively. After the three initial kicks, have Player Y kick from 20, 15 and 10 feet, with Player X defending the goal. Award players one point for each goal made.

Diagram 4.1

Reaction Ball

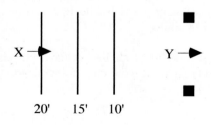

20'   15'   10'

(8) BUTTERFLY FOUR SQUARE

Description

Goals: Practice striking timing and accuracy.
                Incorporate agility into game situation.

Alignment: Standing in Squares I and III (diagonally opposite).

Movements: Sliding, striking one- or two-handed.

Equipment: 8-1/2-inch playground or plastic ball.

Social
   structure: Cooperative.
                2 players, ages 7 to 12.

Directions

Instruct Player X to serve the ball to Square II with a bounce and hit (#1 in Diagram 4.2). Tell Player Y to slide to Square II (dotted line in diagram) and strike the ball diagonally to Square IV. Have Player X move to Square IV and strike the ball to Square III. Have Player Y go back to Square III and strike the ball diagonally to Square I, completing the butterfly pattern. Have players repeat the pattern, counting the number of consecutive hits. Counting starts over when the ball...

1. ...is missed.   3. ...lands out of the proper square.
2. ...lands on a line.   4. ...bounces more than once.

Alternative: Change servers to provide the greatest variety of hits. The server always hits the ball straight across, and the receiver hits it diagonally.

Diagram 4.2

Butterfly Four Square

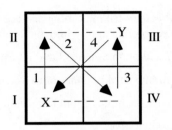

(9) TANDEM TOSS

Description

Goals: Communicate with one another.
              Practice tossing underhand.
              Understand trajectory needed to keep beanbags from
              colliding.

Alignment: Partners standing three feet from their respective ends of a
              tire chain that rests on the floor.

Movements: Tossing underhand.

Equipment: Five bicycle tires, 10 beanbags per person.

Social   Cooperative.
  structure: 2 players, ages 7 to 12.

Directions

Have players toss a beanbag into the closest tire from opposite ends of the
chain (see Diagram 4.3). If a beanbag misses its tire players continue
tossing to the closest tire until both make it in on the same try. When
both beanbags land and remain in the correct tires, have players each toss
a beanbag to their next tires, and so on until one has been tossed into their
last tires (tire #1 for Player Y and tire #5 for Player X). Encourage
players to strategize to prevent beanbags from colliding during later
tosses.

Score the game by the number of successful tandem tosses made. The best score is 5 points regardless how many beanbags are used. (i.e. Players incur no penalty for missing tire) Once players have scored 5 points with the 20 beanbags allotted, they may score ensuing rounds by the number of beanbags remaining when they complete the five tandem tosses. The best score is 10 points, since at least 10 beanbags are required to complete five tandem tosses.

Alternative: For additional challenge, require players to use opposite hands, or to begin the game six feet from their ends of the tire chain.

Diagram 4.3

Tandem Toss

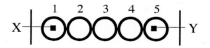

(10) DOWN BALL

Description

Goals:	Practice striking in game situation. Understand angle of trajectory. React to changes in ball trajectory.
Alignment:	Standing facing a wall.
Movements:	Striking.
Equipment:	One playground ball or volleyball, roll of tape.
Social structure:	Competitive. 2 players, ages 8 to 12.

Directions

Place tape marks on a wall to indicate the corners of a rectangle six feet long by three feet high. Begin the rectangle three feet off the floor. Have players stand behind an endline three feet away from the wall opposite the rectangle. Designate one player as the server. Instruct the server to begin play by throwing the ball so it bounces on the floor first and then hits the wall in the rectangle. From then on, instruct players to alternate striking the ball so the opponent misses, with each hit striking the floor first and landing within the rectangle. The last player to successfully hit the ball while following the parameters wins that round. The winner of a given round serves the next round.

Alternatives: Change the distance from the wall, the size of the rectangle, and/or the ball used as necessary.

(11) OUT OF SIGHT

Description

Goals: Cooperate with and trust partner.
            Practice communicating.

Alignment: One partner sitting on scooter; other partner standing
            behind wearing blindfold.

Movements: Pushing.

Equipment: One scooter and blindfold per pair, several cones and
            other miscellaneous equipment.

Social   Cooperative.
  structure: 2 players, ages 8 to 12.

Directions

Set up an obstacle course using cones and other equipment available and
have sets of partners begin at either end of the gym. Have players pretend
they were watching fireworks on a boat; one of the fireworks landed on
the boat, causing an explosion that blinded half the people. Their only
way to safety is to navigate small lifeboats (scooters) across a rocky
channel to shore. Instruct those wearing a blindfold to push their
respective partners through the obstacle course following the verbal
directions of those on scooters. All players can move at the same time,
taking different routes across the channel. Players may score their success
by the time it takes to get across. Add five seconds to a given pair's score
for each obstacle hit. (If scooters bump each other add five seconds to
both pairs.)

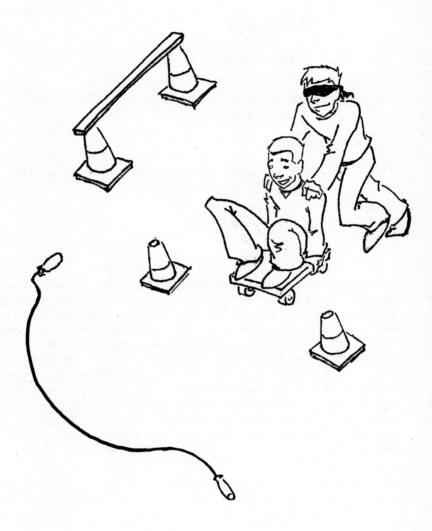

Figure 4.1: Illustration of *Out of Sight*.

(12) KEEPING PACE

Description

Goals: Exercise total body intermittently.
Practice pacing.

Alignment: Standing with partner at chosen starting point.

Movements: Variety of locomotor skills selected by players.

Equipment: Markers to outline playing area, paper, pencil, stopwatch.

Social
structure: Cooperative or competitive.
2 players, ages 8 to 14.

Directions

Instruct players to decide on a route for traveling that would take from one to three minutes to complete. Have Player $\underline{X}$ complete the route using a chosen means of traveling, while Player $\underline{Y}$ keeps time. Have players switch roles so each person has a baseline time recorded. Allow Player $\underline{Y}$ to use a different means of traveling than Player $\underline{X}$. Encourage players to maintain a constant pace, rather than to complete the route quickly.

Competitive version: While alternating roles, have players complete a second and third round trying to get as close as possible to their individual baseline times. Score the game by adding the difference in player's individual times between rounds one and two to the difference in time between rounds two and three. The lower the sum, the better the score.

Cooperative version: Have players add their baseline times for round one. While alternating roles, tell players to complete a second and third round trying to get as close as possible to their joint time for round one. In this version, recommend that Player $\underline{Y}$ try to adjust his pace to offset the error in pacing of Player $\underline{X}$.

Alternative: For additional challenge, require players to use a different means of traveling for each round (not necessarily the same as each other).

(13) SHORT COURT

Description

Goals: Practice striking in game situation.
Improve hand-eye coordination.
Understand ways to vary shot placement.

Alignment: Standing behind the service line on tennis or pickleball courts with four players per court.

Movements: Forehand and backhand striking.

Equipment: One tennis racket or paddle per person, one tennis ball or gator ball per pair.

Social structure: Competitive.
2 players, ages 9 to 14.

Directions

Determine partners and have them stand across from each other behind their respective service lines. Have one player serve the ball into the opposite service box (straight across, not diagonally) with a bounce and hit. Instruct players to alternate hits until one misses with all hits landing within the service box. Rotate partners every three minutes and have players keep their running scores (1 point for each rally won).

Alternative: For older players utilize regular tennis serving rotation and scoring. For younger players utilize shorter paddles and small gator balls.

(14) BACK AND FORCE

Description

Goals: Understand and practice guarding and striking.
Utilize different forces in game situation.

Alignment: Standing facing partner scattered throughout area.

Movements: Guarding, running, striking one-handed.

Equipment: One 10- to 12-inch balloon for every two people.

Social
structure: Competitive.
2 players, ages 9 to 14.

Directions

Have players alternate striking the balloon at an upward or sideward trajectory. Challenge each player to be the last one to touch the balloon before it lands on the floor. Encourage strategies such as hitting the balloon hard away from the opponent, hitting it softly just before it touches the floor, and/or positioning one's body between the balloon and the opponent. Have players begin a new round if the balloon is inadvertently hit downward.

Alternative: For additional challenge, require players to strike the balloon with the nondominant hand only.

(15) BALLOON DESCENT

Description

Goals: Improve body awareness.
                 Understand and practice guarding and striking.

Alignment: Standing facing partner scattered throughout area.

Movements: Guarding, striking one- or two-handed.

Equipment: One 10- to 12-inch balloon per person, partners with
                 different colors.

Social   Competitive.
  structure: 2 players, ages 9 to 14.

Directions

Instruct each player to begin striking a balloon in the air without letting it fall to the ground or coming to rest in the hands or against the body. Allow players to strike with either hand or both simultaneously. While keeping their own balloons in the air, challenge players to make the opponent's balloon land on the floor. This may occur directly by hitting the opponent's balloon downward, or indirectly by standing between the opponent and her balloon.

Chapter 5

Games for Small Groups

G ames for small groups are generally more complex than games
for partners, and less complex than games for large groups.
Although many small group games are more suited to upper
elementary and middle school players, primary school children can
successfully participate, particularly in settings where adults can play
with children. Alignments are more varied than with partner games, since
just two people cannot stand in a circle or square shape, as in *Beach Ball
Bop* (p. 75) and *Clockwise Four Square* (p. 57), respectively. Although
movements and equipment utilized in small group games are not
necessarily more complex than in partner games, players often need to
observe and respond to the play of several other people. This is
particularly true, given that anywhere from 3 to 12 players constitutes a
small group.

Small group games provide a good atmosphere for fostering social
interaction. Input from more than two people is possible, yet players do
not become "lost in the shuffle" as they might in large groups. Leaders
cannot assume players necessarily cooperate just because they are placed
in small groups, however. The input from a given person depends on the
size of the small group, initiative of the person, and receptivity of others.

In addition to group size and initiative, group members may lack
specific cooperative skills needed. In games where group communication
and problem solving are stated goals (i.e. *Invent a Course*, p. 72; *Blanket*

Launch, p. 84), leaders are encouraged to assign specific responsibilities within groups. Assigning responsibilities allows all participants to take an active role. In *Blanket Launch*, for instance, one player can monitor timing of tosses, another can determine if tosses meet stated criteria, and still another can record a score. Over a few trials, all participants can assume one of the responsibilities. Additional roles of players are discussed in chapter 8.

Leaders may vary the way in which small group games are utilized. Some games may be played by large groups of children, breaking them down into multiple groups. *Exchange Ball* (p. 81), for instance, could be used with multiple groups when an entire class needs practice tossing and catching. On the other hand, the equipment required in *Rope Rescue* (p. 76) does not permit playing it with multiple groups. Therefore, it may be played when only a small group is present, or as one station among others within a large class. More specific suggestions for utilizing stations are given in the companion book (Henkel, 2010). In the 32 small group games that follow, the number of players indicated for social structure within the GAMES acronym informs leaders of possible ways to group players.

(16) CLOCKWISE FOUR SQUARE

Description

Goals: Practice striking.
                Improve hand-eye coordination.

Alignment: One player standing in each square.

Movements: Striking one- or two-handed.

Equipment: 8-1/2-inch playground or plastic ball.

Social   Cooperative.
    structure: 3-4 players per group, ages 5 to 8.

Directions

Instruct Player W to serve the ball to Player X with a bounce and a hit (#1 in Diagram 5.1). Tell other players to continue hitting the ball clockwise, letting it bounce after each hit (#2-4 in diagram). Have players keep score by counting the number of consecutive hits until the ball (a) is missed, (b) lands on a line, or (c) lands out of the proper square. When three people play, the ball travels in the path of a triangle between three squares (depicted on right side of diagram).

Alternatives: For variety, have players reverse the path of the ball to practice receiving it from the other direction. For additional challenge, have players hit the ball with their nondominant hands only and/or hit the ball as many times as possible in a specified time frame.

Diagram 5.1

Clockwise Four Square

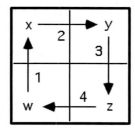 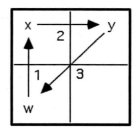

(17) LOOP DA HOOP

Description

Goals: Communicate with others.
                Solve a problem.
                Utilize flexibility.

Alignment: Standing in a circle facing the center.

Movements: Balancing, bending, grasping, stretching.

Equipment: One or two hoops.

Social   Cooperative or cooperative within competitive.
  structure: 5-10 players per group, ages 5 and up.

Directions

Instruct players to hold hands in a circle with a hoop hanging between two people. On signal, tell the group to pass the hoop around the circle without letting any hands go. Encourage players to try different strategies to help their neighbors position the hoop. The task is finished when the hoop returns to its initial position. With seven or more players, add a second hoop across from the first hoop. Once a group has completed the task, score the cooperative version by how many hoops a group can pass around the circle in a specified time frame (passing the same hoop[s] around multiple times until time expires). Score the cooperative within competitive version by comparing the times of two or more groups.

Alternative: For additional challenge, suggest that players try to pass the hoops without letting them touch the floor.

Figure 5.1: Illustration of *Loop da Hoop*.

(18) MONKEY ON A ROPE

Description

Goals:　　　　Practice passing and catching.
Communicate with others.

Alignment:　　Standing inside bicycle tires forming a circle around suspended rope.

Movements:　Catching, grasping, passing two-handed, swinging.

Equipment:　Two different colored playground balls, one tire per person, rope suspended from ceiling or tree.

Social
structure:　Cooperative.
5-8 players, ages 7 to 10.

Directions

Give a ball to two players who are not "neighbors." On signal, tell each player to pass the ball using two hands to someone else in the circle. Options for Player F are indicated by lines in Diagram 5.2. Allow passes to bounce once or travel through the air. Challenge players to continue making as many passes as possible during one minute, individually monitoring their scores. Award the group one point for each pass caught (sum of individual scores), as long as (a) people pass to players who are not immediate neighbors, (b) people passing and receiving the ball keep at least one foot inside their tires, and (c) passes do not hit the suspended rope (darkened circle in Diagram 5.2).

If one or more of the rules is violated, have the person who passed the ball get the rope and return to her tire. Have that player become a "monkey on a rope" by swinging to someone else's tire (besides an immediate neighbor) and touching her feet down inside that tire. Then that player in turn swings to the empty tire. If both balls are involved in a violation, then instruct both players who passed the balls to exchange with another player on the rope before passes resume.

Alternative: For additional challenge, have players swing the rope prior to beginning the ball exchange so it acts as a moving obstacle.

Diagram 5.2
Monkey on a Rope

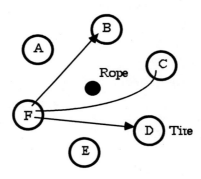

Diagram 5.3
Four Square Rotation

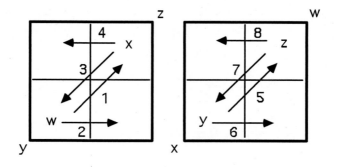

(19) FOUR SQUARE ROTATION

Description

Goals: Exercise total body continuously.
                    Practice striking two-handed.

Alignment: Two players standing in diagonally opposite squares; one
                    player standing behind each of the other players, outside
                    the squares.

Movements: Running, striking two-handed.

Equipment: 8-1/2-inch playground or plastic ball.

Social   Cooperative.
    structure: 4 players per group, ages 7 to 11.

Directions

Have Player W serve the ball to Player X with a bounce and a two-hand
hit (#1 in Diagram 5.3). Then have Player W run to the right (#2 in
diagram) around the opposite square and line up in Player Z's position.
While Player W is running, tell Player X to hit the ball to Player Y (#3)
and run around the opposite square and line up in Player Y's original
position. Count the number of consecutive hits until the ball (a) is
missed, (b) bounces twice, or (c) lands on a line or out of bounds.

(20) CENTIPEDE

Description

Goals: Respect and trust others.
Improve agility.

Alignment: Sitting, kneeling, or laying on a scooter behind a line in any formation.

Movements: Grasping, scooting.

Equipment: One scooter per person.

Social
  structure: Cooperative.
4-8 players per group, ages 7 to 11.

Directions

Challenge players to advance their scooters to the other side of the playing area (about 30 feet) while remaining linked in some way. If the centipede breaks apart at any moment, have players begin again from behind the initial line. Score the game based on distance or by time. In the former case, award 25 points for having all scooters cross each quarter of the playing area:

All scooters make it 1/4 of the way = 25 points.
All scooters make it 1/2 of the way = 50 points.
All scooters make it 3/4 of the way = 75 points.
Everyone in group crosses the endline = 100 points.

Score the game based on time after groups make it across the endline once successfully. Time successive attempts and see if a given group can beat its own score.

Alternative: Repeat the activity with all group members in a different position on the scooter.

(21) ALIVE AND KICKIN'

Description

Goals: Respect other people's spaces.
                Practice reacting to ball quickly.

Alignment: Lying down in a circle facing the center.

Movements: Kicking two-footed, pushing.

Equipment: 36- or 48-inch beach ball.

Social   Cooperative.
   structure: 8-12 players per group, ages 7 to 11.

Directions

Designate one "rover" for every three players. Instruct all players except the rovers to hold hands and form a circle. Have circle players drop hands and lay down on their backs with their feet toward the center, lifted off the floor. Tell rovers to stand outside the circle, facing the center. Toss the beach ball toward the feet of the circle players. Challenge circle players to keep the ball "alive" by kicking it as many times as possible. When the ball leaves the circle, have rovers hit or push it back toward a kicker to continue the sequence. Award one point for each consecutive kick without letting the ball stop or land on the floor. Rotate rovers as time allows.

Note: Have circle players remove eyeglasses to avoid possible injury.

Alternative: If the kicks of the group are difficult to count, score the game based on time by monitoring how long the ball remains moving off the floor.

(22) HUMAN MACHINERY

Description

Goals: Communicate with others.
Understand foundational movement concepts.
Improve body awareness.

Alignment: Standing facing other group members.

Movements: Variety of movements selected by groups.

Equipment: None.

Social
  structure: Cooperative.
4-8 players per group, ages 7 to 12.

Directions

Challenge players to use their bodies to make a "human machine" with everyone attached in some way. Machines must satisfy a group of specific characteristics. Examples include, but are not limited to:

1. One body part moving slowly; one part moving quickly.
2. One body part moving at a low level; one part moving at a high level.
3. One moving part central to the body (i.e. head, shoulders, trunk, hips); one moving part peripheral to the body (i.e. fingers, hands, wrist, toes, feet, ankles).

Allow players to fulfill characteristics of machines separately or jointly. For instance, a person's head may move slowly at a high level. When one machine is completed, encourage players to satisfy the same characteristics in different ways. Award points for task completion and for creativity. Determine creativity points by the name, shape and sound effects of the machine.

Alternatives: Increase or decrease task difficulty by adding to, or subtracting from, the number of required characteristics, respectively. For variety, change the type of required characteristics in the machine (i.e. one body part moving under another; one body part moving over another).

Figure 5.2: Illustration of *Human Machinery*.

(23) BARREL BALL

Description

Goals: Communicate with others.
Practice striking one-handed.
Practice sequencing.

Alignment: Standing facing one another two steps away from barrel; tape a circle on the floor around the barrel one step away.

Movements: Striking one-handed.

Equipment: 8-1/2-inch nerf or plastic ball, one paddle per person, large barrel or garbage can.

Social
  structure: Cooperative.
3-6 players per group, ages 7 to 12.

Directions

Instruct players to strike the ball amongst themselves in the air using their hands. Tell players to strike the ball into the barrel with each player hitting the ball before scoring. Allow the same person to strike the ball more than once, but not twice in succession. With younger players, score the game by task completion, or successfully having each person hit the ball before it lands in the barrel. With older players, score the game by the number of rounds required to have each player make the last hit before the ball goes in the barrel (minimum of three rounds for three players). A round consists of a successful sequence in which a new player makes the last hit, or an unsuccessful sequence that results in one of the following:

1. The ball hits the floor.
2. A player crosses the taped circle.
3. The same player hits the ball twice in a row.
4. The ball goes in the barrel before each person hits it.

Alternative: For more challenge, have players strike the ball with a paddle and/or move the restraining line further from the barrel.

68   *Success for Kids in Active Games*

(24) LOST IN SPACE

Description

Goals: Respect and trust others.
              Strengthen arms.

Alignment: Standing in a circle with each person inside a tire.

Movements: Grasping, swinging.

Equipment: One bicycle tire for each person, rope suspended from
              ceiling or tree in center of tire circle.

Social   Cooperative.
  structure: 5-9 players, ages 7 to 12.

Directions

Have each tire represent a planet, and the rope represents oxygen (darkened circle in Diagram 5.4). Designate the person at planet earth as the initial "rescuer." Have the rescuer swing to any other planet trying to carry oxygen to the stranded astronaut. The mission is successful if the rescuer can (a) name a new planet, and (b) touch down inside the new tire without touching the floor outside the tire. Following "unsuccessful" missions, require the astronaut to attempt the rescue again. Allow the astronaut being rescued to help by grabbing the rescuer as she comes.

Have each rescued astronaut change places with the initial rescuer on the rope. Tell the new rescuer to swing to another planet carrying oxygen. Repeat the sequence until all planets have been reached, and the last astronaut returns to earth. Score the game by the number of swings on the rope required to complete the circuit (minimum number of swings is equal to the number of players). Once players achieve the minimum number of swings, suggest that they try to complete the circuit more quickly.

Alternative: For less challenge, have an extra astronaut begin at earth (two people inside that tire). This gives assistance to the initial rescuer leaving, and to the last astronaut returning to earth.

Diagram 5.4
Lost in Space

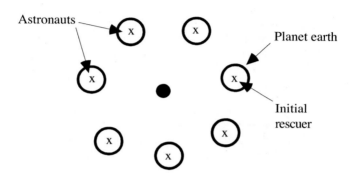

Astronauts

X X

Planet earth

X X

Initial
rescuer

X X

X

(25) FRUIT OF THE ROOM

Description

Goals: Classify fruit and other selected items.
Practice tossing and catching.
Understand need to toss ball quickly, yet accurately.

Alignment: Sitting in a circle facing the center.

Movements: "Bopping," catching, passing.

Equipment: 8-1/2-inch playground or plastic ball, two regular adult
socks stuffed inside a knee sock (with a knot tied to
keep the socks in place).

Social   Competitive.
  structure: 6-9 players per group, ages 7 to 12.

Directions

Designate a tagger to sit in the center of the circle holding the knee sock. Give the ball to a player on the circle. Instruct that player to say the name of a fruit and then pass the ball to another player. Tell each player receiving the ball to name another fruit and release the ball, without repeating the same fruit during the same round. Have the tagger try to follow the path of the ball and "bop" someone with the stuffed sock below the shoulders before that player can release the ball. Have the tagger change places with a circle player when one of the following situations occurs:

1. The tagger bops a player before he releases the ball.
2. A circle player passes an uncatchable ball.
3. A circle player fails to catch the ball.
4. A circle player repeats the name of a fruit during that round.

To avoid disagreements, have the tagger decide whether an error is due to the pass or catch. Consider a ball that hits the tagger a passing error automatically. Score one point for each time a given player goes to the center (points are undesirable).

Alternatives: For variety, provide different items for players to classify (i.e. colors, months, vegetables). For additional challenge, require that no pass be returned directly to the same person who previously had the ball.

(26) SNAP TO IT

Description

Goals: Practice hiking and catching football.
Exercise total body intermittently.
Understand need to hike ball quickly, yet accurately.

Alignment: Each player standing at a different corner of the group's square.

Movements: Catching and hiking football, jogging.

Equipment: One youth football per group, four cones or polydots per group.

Social structure: Competitive.
3 players per group, ages 7-12.

Directions

Form groups of three players. Give each group four cones or polydots to lay in a square on the floor, with corners four to six steps apart. Position players at different corners of their respective group squares. On signal, instruct Player 1 (P1) to snap the ball to Player 2 (P2), indicated by a solid arrow in Diagram 5.5. Then have Player 1 jog ahead to the unoccupied corner (indicated by dotted arrow). Have Player 2 hike the ball to Player 3 and jog to the corner vacated by Player 1 (indicated by like arrows). Have players continue the pattern, trying to catch as many snaps as possible in a specified time (approximately 2-3 minutes). Any snap that is dropped does not count toward a group's total.

Alternative: Substitute any other skill and corresponding equipment to practice passing and receiving in a different manner (i.e. basketball chest pass or soccer pass).

Diagram 5.5
Snap To It

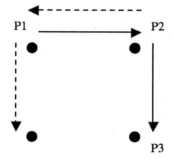

(27) INVENT A COURSE

Description

Goals: Communicate with others.
                Solve problem.
                Practice selected motor skills and abilities.

Alignment: Determined by the group.

Movements: Variety of movements selected by groups.

Equipment: Distributed by leader to each group.

Social   Cooperative set-up, independent play.
  structure: 3-6 players per group, ages 7 to 12.

Directions

Determine groups and send each to a designated location where equipment is waiting.   Provide different equipment for each group. Instruct groups to incorporate their equipment into an obstacle course with the following parameters:

1. Select at least three safe movements or motor skills to perform.
2. Select movements that involve the whole body.
3. Provide a choice of movements somewhere in the course.

Have each group briefly discuss (a) what movements to use, and (b) how to use equipment. Through trial and error, have groups set up an obstacle course for others to try.   If desired, assign specific group roles to participants as suggested in chapter 8.   When the courses are ready, tell one member from each group to remain at his "home" course to explain it, while the rest of the groups rotate to the next course.   In the second rotation, have a different group member return home to explain the activity to the next group (and so on).   Rotate groups to as many courses as time allows.

Note: Although Figure 5.3 includes a ball to indicate variety, courses are best distinguished from *Invent a Game* (p. 74) by disallowing object control movements.

Figure 5.3: Illustration of *Invent a Course*.

(28) INVENT A GAME

Description

Goals: Communicate with others.
              Practice selected movements or motor skills.
              Understand relationship between various game elements.

Alignment: Determined by groups.

Movements: Variety of movements selected by groups.

Equipment: Distributed by leader to each group.

Social   Cooperative set-up, cooperative or competitive play.
  structure: 3-6 players per group, ages 7 to 14.

Directions

Determine groups and send each to a designated location where equipment is waiting. Provide different equipment for each group. Instruct groups to incorporate their equipment into a game with the following parameters:

1. Design games for six players.
2. All people need to be active most of the time.
3. Incorporate at least one object control movement.
4. Provide a choice of movements for players somehow.

Have each group briefly discuss (a) what movements to use, and (b) how to use equipment. Through trial and error, have groups set up a game for others to play. If desired, assign specific group roles to participants as suggested in chapter 8. When the games are ready, tell one member from each group to remain at her "home" game to explain it, while the rest of the groups rotate to the next game. In the second rotation, have a different group member return home to explain it to the next group (and so on). Rotate groups to as many games as time allows.

Note: Along with a different social structure, requiring at least one object control movement helps distinguish invented games from *Invent a Course* (p. 72).

(29) BEACH BALL BOP

Description

Goals: Practice striking in game situation.
                Improve sense of timing.

Alignment: Standing in a circle facing the center with equal
                spacing between players.

Movements: Striking one- or two-handed.

Equipment: One 36- or 48-inch beach ball per group, one polydot
                per player.

Social   Cooperative.
   structure: 5-9 players per circle, ages 7 to 14.

Directions

Form multiple circles, with the players in each circle standing on a polydot. Challenge players to hit (or "bop") the beach ball with their hands as many times as possible without letting it land on the floor, and without the same person hitting it twice in a row. Allow players to step off their dots with one foot at a time to reach the ball. Award the group 25 points for hitting the ball as many times as there are people. Give 50 points for hitting the ball twice as many times as there are people in the group. Continue adding 25 points for each multiple of hits (i.e. three times the number of group members equals 75 points).

Alternative: For additional challenge, utilize a 24-inch beach ball and/or expand the circles with the dots and double all scores.

(30) ROPE RESCUE

Description

Goals: Respect and trust others.
                    Improve upper arm strength.

Alignment: One player laying on back behind near endline; other
                    players standing in a line beyond far endline.

Movements: Grasping, tugging.

Equipment: Tug-of-war rope.

Social   Cooperative.
   structure: 5-8 players, ages 7 to 14.

Directions

Instruct the person lying down ("injured party") to grasp the rope with two hands. Tell other players to hold the rope at waist level and pull hand-over-hand to "rescue" their teammate. Do not have players walk while holding the rope. The teammate is rescued when his entire body crosses the far endline (about 30 feet).

Time how long it takes to complete the rescue. Try the game again with each person as the injured party. Encourage older players to record all scores and determine the average time.

Note: If pulling teammates across the floor causes too much friction, have players pull teammates across a large plastic tarp taped to the floor.

(31) JAM JUMPING

Description

Goals:	Respect and trust others.
	Exercise total body intermittently.
	Practice entering jump rope.
	Improve rhythmical ability.
Alignment:	Standing next to rope facing the same direction; two players ready to twirl rope.
Movements:	Jumping, twirling.
Equipment:	One 25- to 30-foot jumprope per group.
Social structure:	Cooperative.
	6-12 players per group, ages 8 to 12.

Directions

Challenge jumpers "inside" the rope to "jump in a jam" with as many teammates as possible. Award points for the number of people continuously jumping for 5 or 10 seconds, depending on experience of jumpers. Start counting seconds after all players are jumping:

3 people = 25 points.
5 people = 50 points.
7 people = 75 points.
9 people =100 points.

Alternatives: For additional challenge, have players enter the rope through the "front door" and jump for 5 or 10 seconds. Double the scores above for the respective number of people. For still more challenge, have players enter the rope through the "back door" and jump for 5 or 10 seconds. Triple the original scores for the respective number of people.

(32) FLEECE AND FLEE

Description

Goals: Communicate with others.
                Utilize catching and throwing in game situation.

Alignment: Sitting on scooters scattered throughout playing area.

Movements: Catching, scooting, tagging, throwing overhand,
                tossing underhand.

Equipment: Fleece (yarn) ball, two different colored jerseys, one
                scooter per person, markers to outline playing area.

Social   Cooperation within competition.
    structure: 6-10 players per group, ages 8 to 12.

Directions

Instruct all players to sit on a scooter, wearing different colored jerseys to designate teams. Have the team with the yarn ball exchange it back and forth among themselves as many times as possible while trying to flee from the other team. Do not allow the defensive team to make physical contact with the fleers except for tagging purposes. Award the fleers one point for each consecutive catch. Have teams change roles (and, therefore, start over counting) when one of the following conditions occurs:

1. The defensive team retrieves a loose ball.
2. The defensive team intercepts the ball.
3. The defensive team tags a fleer who has the ball.
4. One of the fleers leaves the boundaries.
5. One of the fleers throws the ball out of bounds.

Alternative: For additional challenge, require the yarn ball to be thrown to a different player than the person who last had possession.

(33) BINGO BOWLING

Description

Goals: Practice rolling in game situation.
              Understand and practice bowling footwork.
              Exhibit cooperation while setting pins with others.

Alignment: Standing in small groups, with one person bowling, a
              scorer on deck, and two pinsetters.

Movements: Rolling.

Equipment: 10 plastic bowling pins and one rubber bowling ball
              per group.

Social   Cooperative within competitive.
  structure: 4 players per group, ages 8 to 12.

Directions

Organize groups at lanes and distribute *Bingo Bowling* cards and pencils
(example of card in Figure 5.4). Naturally, additional cards are needed
with numbers arranged differently. Instruct players to assume initial roles
outlined above under alignment. Have players bowl until they complete a
bingo vertically, horizontally or diagonally. A turn consists of just one
roll, since the number of fallen pins needed varies.

Alternatives: Utilize other patterns on the cards, such as four corners and
blackout, depending on time allotted.

4	7	8	9	5
7	9	2	6	1
8	3	FREE	2	4
3	4	6	5	8
6	5	1	7	3

Figure 5.4: Illustration of *Bingo Bowling* Card.

(34) EXCHANGE BALL

Description

Goals: Practice passing and catching.
Exercise total body intermittently.

Alignment: Standing on polydots arranged in a circle.

Movements: Catching, dodging, running, passing, tagging.

Equipment: One foam ball, football, or playground ball.

Social   Competitive.
   structure: 5-8 players per group, ages 8 to 12.

Directions

Position players on polydots arranged in a circle (size of circle depends on number of players). Position the tagger in the middle of the circle. On signal, players travel inside dots anywhere they wish. While traveling, players exchange the ball by tossing and catching with their hands without returning it to the same person the ball was received from. As players exchange the ball, the tagger tries to tag the person holding the ball. If successful, the tagger changes places with the one tagged. If a tag has not occurred before the ball hits the floor, the last player to touch it before it falls changes places with the tagger. Any player who stops moving through space while the ball is being exchanged must change places with the tagger.

(35) THE FLY

Description

Goals: Improve hand-eye coordination.
                    Practice reacting quickly to ball.

Alignment: Standing in a line abreast, facing the leader, who is 8-10
                    feet away.

Movements: Catching, passing.

Equipment: One playground ball or volleyball.

Social   Competitive.
    structure: 4-6 players, ages 8 to 12.

Directions

Instruct players in the line to clasp their own hands together. Tell the leader to pass the ball in the air to someone in the line. Tell that player to catch the ball, return it in the same manner, and re-clasp her hands. Award a line player a "fly," or point for each catch. Encourage the leader to occasionally fake a pass to tempt a line player to unclasp hands unnecessarily. When this occurs, subtract one fly from the player who makes the error. Also subtract a fly for an accurate pass that is dropped. Do not penalize players for failing to catch an inaccurate pass. Have leaders make the determination regarding accuracy of passes. Appoint players who earn five flies as the new leader. Adjust the distance between the leader and group as necessary.

Note: The larger the group and/or the less time available, the more need to rotate leaders when a player earns fewer flies.

(36) CORNER BALL

Description

Goals: Practice throwing and catching in game situation.
Improve movement without the ball.

Alignment: Standing scattered throughout playing area.

Movements: Throwing, catching, tagging, dodging.

Equipment: One nerf or gator ball per group, cones to outline area.

Social   Cooperative within competitive.
   structure: 6-8 players per group, ages 8 to 13.

Directions

Arrange players in groups of about seven and position each group in its marked area (about one fourth of gym). Designate two taggers per group and give one of the taggers a nerf ball or gator ball. On signal, instruct taggers to tag others in their groups by touching them with the ball (not throwing it). Runners and taggers may go anywhere in their areas, but taggers may take only one step while holding the ball. This requires taggers to "corner" the others and then receive a pass close enough to tag someone.

Score the game by the number of players tagged in three minutes, before rotating taggers (more is better). Individuals may also keep track of the number of times they are tagged across multiple rounds (fewer is better). In either case, any player tagged remains in the game, but may not be tagged again until another player is tagged.

(37) BLANKET LAUNCH

Description

Goals: Communicate with others.
                Solve problem.
                Improve sense of timing.

Alignment: Standing around blanket, equally spaced, facing middle.

Movements: Cushioning, lifting.

Equipment: One blanket and playground ball per group.

Social   Cooperative.
   structure: 4-7 players per group, ages 8 to 14.

Directions

Instruct players to grasp the edge of a blanket, holding it waist high. With the ball in the center of the blanket, have players "launch" it vertically in the air and catch it. Tell the group to repeat the launch and catch as many times as possible, with each launch going higher than the previous one (players begin with a low toss). Allow the ball to come to a stop between tosses. Require the group to begin again when one of the following conditions occurs:

1. The ball lands on the floor.
2. A player touches the ball.
3. A launch does not go higher than the previous one.

Alternative: For variety, challenge players to repeat the game with each toss going lower than the previous one (players begin with a high toss).

Figure 5.5: Illustration of *Blanket Launch*.

(38) ADVANTAGE

Description

Goals: Practice basketball skills in game situation.
                Exercise total body intermittently.

Alignment: Offensive players standing with the ball at half
                court; one more player on offense than on defense.

Movements: Dribbling, guarding, passing, rebounding, shooting.

Equipment: Child or youth basketball.

Social   Cooperative within competitive, independent scoring.
  structure: 3, 5, or 7 players, ages 8 to 14.

Directions

Instruct offensive players to use their "advantage" of having an extra offensive player to score a basket. When a basket is made, award each offensive player a point, and have the same players begin with the ball from half court again. Tell defensive players to intercept the ball or get a rebound to prevent a score. When this occurs have that defensive player change places with the offensive player who last touched the ball. Have the new offensive team take the ball back to half court and begin a new turn.

When the ball goes out of bounds, allow the current offensive team to retain possession, since no defensive player actually had the ball under control. Restrict the same offensive players to scoring three times consecutively. When this occurs, have the oldest offensive player automatically change places with the youngest defensive player. Have players individually keep track of their running scores.

Note: Substitute a soccer ball or floor hockey equipment for the basketball, in order to practice passing and shooting with feet or sticks, respectively.

(39) PASS 'N MOVE

Description

Goals: Practice soccer skills in game situation.
Exercise total body intermittently.

Alignment: Three players standing in triangle; one in the middle.

Movements: Dribbling, guarding, passing, trapping.

Equipment: Soccer ball, four cones.

Social
   structure: Cooperative within competitive.
4 players per group, ages 8 to 14.

Directions

Place cones in a square formation about five yards apart at the corners. Position players near three of the cones, with a fourth player in the middle as a defender (#'s 1-4 in Diagram 5.6). Offensive players support the one with the ball by giving him two targets for passing. When a Player has the ball near Cone A, teammates should be near cones B and D. When the ball is passed to Player 2, Player 3 should move near cone C. Defenders earn their way out of the middle by just contacting the ball, or by changing places with someone who makes an error in passing or receiving the ball. Score the game by the number of times players serve as the defender (not counting the first appointed time). Points are undesirable.

Note: Substitute floor hockey equipment for the soccer ball, in order to practice passing and trapping with sticks.

Diagram 5.6

Pass 'n Move

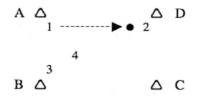

(40) DISC GOLF

Description

Goals: Improve hand-eye coordination.
                Improve sense of aim.
                Extend courtesy to others.

Alignment: Standing in a line at the first "tee."

Movements: Throwing sidearm, walking.

Equipment: One Frisbee or disc per person or partners may alternate
                throws if necessary; equipment for holes as needed.

Social   Competitive and cooperative.
  structure: 3-5 players per group, ages 8 and up.

Directions

Divide players into small groups and assign each group to a different starting hole. Give members in the same group different colored discs. Designate one member per group as a scorer, and give each scorer a pencil and scorecard (made in advance) that reflects the location and sequence of holes. A variety of holes make a course more interesting. Holes may be designated by landmarks on the property (i.e. tree, backstop), or by recreation equipment (i.e. soccer goal or tire on ground). Holes may also be determined by spray painting a target on the ground or a small portion of a large landmark (i.e. backstop). The exact choice of holes is less important than clarity in identifying them.

Instruct each group to begin play by taking turns throwing the discs toward its initial hole. All subsequent throws need to occur in sequence so that discs furthest from the hole are thrown before closer discs. Players with discs closer to the hole need to remain behind peers throwing discs that are further to prevent entering the flight path of discs. This requires ongoing courtesy and patience similar to regular golf etiquette. Often a couple throws may occur simultaneously for the sake of time and activity. For instance, when two discs are approximately the same distance from the hole, they may both be thrown together without danger to others.

(41) SIDE-BY-SIDE

Description

Goals: Understand how to coordinate movement with other people to solve a problem.
Cooperate with others.
Extend courtesy to others.

Alignment: Standing in a line "side-by-side" facing the same direction.

Movements: Balancing, walking.

Equipment: None.

Social structure: Cooperative.
4-9 players per group, ages 8 and up.

Directions

Instruct players in each group to make contact with their neighbor's feet in some way, such as pressing shoes sideways or placing one foot on top of another (the two end people contact only one teammate's foot). Challenge groups to advance as far as possible without losing contact with each other's feet. When that occurs, have the group begin again from the starting point.

One way to measure progress is to simply record how far each group can advance. When a group starts over, challenge it to improve its former score. A second way to measure progress is to monitor how long it takes to reach a specified distance. This option is only viable when a group has demonstrated a high level of success.

Note: The younger the age, the more need to begin with fewer people per line and add people only after groups demonstrate success.

(42) SEQUENCE

Description

Goals: Practice throwing and catching in game situation.
                Exercise total body intermittently.

Alignment: Scattered in large square or rectangle.

Movements: Catching, guarding, passing.

Equipment: One Frisbee or disc, four cones, pinnies for one team.

Social   Cooperative within competitive.
  structure: 4-7 players per group, ages 9 and up.

Directions

Determine two teams and disperse pinnies to one team. Instruct players to match up with opponents so each person guards another one-on-one. Give Team X possession of the disc. Have that team pass the disc among teammates as many times as possible without missing. Passes may be numbered out loud so everyone knows the score. The first pass is uncontested. Subsequent passes may not be thrown to the same person the disc is received from. A miss occurs when the disc is dropped, thrown out of bounds, or intercepted by the opponent. When that occurs, Team Y begins a sequence. Players may not strip the disc from an opponent. Players are limited to two steps while holding the disc, so that most movement occurs without possession.

Each team tries to better its own longest running sequence. When multiple teams are present, rotate teams between courts and instruct the team with the shortest sequence on each court to begin the next game.

Note: A "sequence" refers to the number of uninterrupted passes, rather than to a particular order or location of passes.

Alternative: Substitute a football of appropriate size for the disc.

(43) SOCCER SEQUENCE

Description

Goals: Practice soccer skills in game situation.
Exercise total body intermittently.

Alignment: Standing on perimeter of square; specified players beginning in center of square.

Movements: Dribbling, guarding, passing, trapping.

Equipment: Soccer ball, eight cones, pinnies for one team.

Social
structure: Cooperative within competitive.
6-9 players per group, ages 9 and up.

Directions

Position eight players around the perimeter of a square, alternating teams, as shown in Diagram 5.7. Perimeter players must stay on one half of a given side, marked by cones. Start remaining players inside the square to run wherever they wish. The more players in the middle, the larger the square needs to be. Instruct a sideline player from Team X to begin a sequence by passing the ball to any teammate. The first pass is uncontested. Team X continues to pass the ball among teammates as many times as possible without Team Y touching the ball (possible sequence indicated by arrows in diagram). When Team Y touches the ball, or when Team X kicks it out of bounds, Team Y begins a sequence starting with the nearest sideline player. Rotate new players to the middle intermittently. Each team tries to better its own longest running sequence.

Note: A "sequence" refers to the number of uninterrupted passes, rather than to a particular order or location of passes.

Diagram 5.7

Soccer Sequence

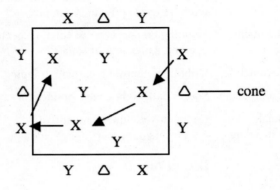

cone

Diagram 5.8

Jugglemania

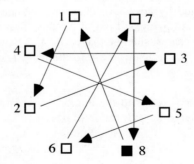

(44) JUGGLEMANIA

Description

Goals: Improve hand-eye coordination.
Improve sense of timing.
Practice concentrating.

Alignment: Standing in a circle facing the center.

Movements: Catching, tossing underhand.

Equipment: One yarn or tennis ball for every two people.

Social
structure: Cooperative.
6-9 players per group, ages 9 and up.

Directions

Designate a leader to put balls in play (Player 8 in Diagram 5.8). Instruct the leader to toss a ball across the circle to someone else. Tell players to continue tossing the ball until all have caught it, without tossing it to a neighbor, and without tossing it to the same person twice. Numbers in the diagram illustrate one possible sequence. Have players repeat the sequence until they know it well. Then have the leader toss additional balls into the sequence gradually. Recommend that players concentrate only on the people they toss balls to, and the people they receive balls from. Challenge players to "juggle" a given number of balls as long as possible.

(45) TOXIC TREATS

Description

Goals: Understand how to coordinate movement with other
                people to solve a problem.
                Cooperate with others.
                Communicate with others.

Alignment: Standing in a group behind a restraining line.

Movements: Balancing, stepping.

Equipment: One base for every two people.

Social   Cooperative.
  structure: 6-10 players per group, ages 9 and up.

Directions

Instruct players to rescue themselves by moving across a 30-foot span based on the following scenario. Encourage players to talk about options and help each other in any way that does not violate the guidelines.

Suppose you all work the late shift at a chocolate factory. A toxic chemical leaked into the water in a mote that surrounds the factory. You need to cross the mote soon, because the factory may explode. The only chocolate that is not contaminated is a handful of square wafers (i.e. bases). Since the bridge across the mote was taken out in a storm, the wafers are the only means of crossing the mote. The wafers are strong enough to support your weight, but they will float away if you lose contact with them on the floor at any time (i.e. if a player takes her hand off even for a moment while placing one on the floor, remove that wafer; wafers may be handed off or tossed, however). If anyone touches the water, she must begin from the original side again.

Alternative: Utilizing the same scenario, replace the bases with a large tarp. Have players (8-12) spread out the tarp and begin by standing along the near end. In a similar manner, the group's only safe passage across the mote is via the tarp, without any body part touching the water. One solution is to fold the tarp over in the middle, shift to the other side, then unfold the near end from underneath.

(46) ONE-CATCH VOLLEYBALL

Description

Goals: Practice striking.
Improve hand-eye coordination.

Alignment: Standing in rows on two sides of volleyball court.

Movements: Striking one- and two-handed.

Equipment: Youth, or oversized volleyball.

Social
    structure: Competitive.
8-12 players per group, ages 10 to 14.

Directions

Have players begin with an underhand serve. From then on, require teams to touch the ball at least two times, or the ball goes to the other team. Each time the ball crosses the net, have the first player catch it and toss it in the air on that side of the net. Require subsequent players to hit the ball as in volleyball, with unlimited hits. At the end of each rally one team scores a point, regardless who served (rally scoring). Each time either team earns a side out, have both teams rotate clockwise, enabling all players to change positions more frequently than in regular volleyball.

Alternatives: For variety, allow teams to play or catch the ball off the bounce once every time the ball comes to their side.

(47) FRISBEE FRENZY

Description

Goals: Practice throwing.
               Improve hand-eye coordination.

Alignment: Standing in tire in square or circle formation.

Movements: Throwing one-handed.

Equipment: Two Frisbees or discs of different colors, one bicycle tire
               per person.

Social   Cooperative.
structure: 5-7 players per group, ages 10 to 14.

Directions

Set up tires in a square or circle formation, depending on number of
players, with an additional tire in the middle. Have each player stand in a
tire. Give one disc to the middle player and the other disc to any
perimeter player. Instruct players to exchange discs back and forth with
the following parameters:

1. One colored disc may be thrown between perimeter players only
   (i.e. "perimeter disc").
2. The other disc may be exchanged back and forth between the
   middle player and any perimeter player only (i.e. "middle disc").

Players score a point for each disc caught with at least one foot inside
their respective tires. Players may monitor points individually and then
total them after a given number of rounds. Blow a whistle at one-minute
intervals to signal the following changes between rounds:

1. Return discs to their initial locations. If caught, they result in a
   point as with other exchanges.
2. Have the player with the perimeter disc change places with the
   middle player.
3. Reverse roles of the disc, so the disc initially reserved for
   perimeter play now becomes the middle disc.

Chapter 6

Games for Large Groups

L arge group games are the most complex, since the amount and variety of activity generally increases with the number of players in a game. Large groups most often contain 15 to 30 players, although *Raindrops* (p. 103) may be played with as few as 8 players, and *Topsy Turvy* (p. 104) with 40 or more players. Games with as many as 30 or 40 players are recommended only when leaders are confident that all participants can have an active role and remain safe.

Alignments are still more varied than with small group games, but movements and equipment utilized are not necessarily more complex. Since more large group games are competitive compared to partner and small group games, the social climate may be more intense. Leaders need to be aware of individual performances, because the skills of any given player are displayed in front of more peers. Leaders can then monitor peer responses to one another so players are built up, rather than torn down, through game experiences. Even if winning is not emphasized during large group games, the psychological maturity required is best suited to older elementary and middle school players. Yet, primary level children can succeed in some of the activities, especially in settings where adults can participate with them.

(48) MUSICAL HOOPS

Description

Goals:	Respect and trust others.
	Practice rhythmical expression.
	Problem solve.
Alignment:	Standing scattered on basketball or volleyball court, depending on number of players.
Movements:	Variety of locomotor skills.
Equipment:	Boom box, music, one hoop for every three people.
Social structure:	Cooperative.
	12-30 players, ages 5 to 8.

Directions

Scatter hoops evenly throughout the playing area. When the music begins, have players travel on their feet any way they choose without touching or stepping in a hoop. When the music stops, tell all players to get inside a hoop. The same hoop may have anywhere from zero to several players, as long as everyone is entirely inside some hoop (with whatever body parts touch the floor).

For each additional round remove one (10-20 players) or two (21-30 players) hoops. Encourage players to vary the tempo and means of traveling. As the number of hoops decreases, encourage players to help each other and creatively maximize space inside remaining hoops. Score the game by how few hoops remain with all players still fitting inside.

Note: To maintain safety with larger groups, exclude running as one of the movement options.

Alternatives: Select music with a clear theme for movers, such as the *William Tell Overture* (horses galloping), *Monster Mash* (scary movements), or *In the Hall of the Mountain King* (light, sneaking movements).

Figure 6.1: Illustration of *Musical Hoops*.

(49) HEADS UP

Description

Goals:	Help others.
	Practice balancing.
Alignment:	Standing scattered throughout area.
Movements:	Balancing, squatting, walking.
Equipment:	One beanbag per person, markers to outline area.
Social	Cooperative.
structure:	8-30 players, ages 5 to 8.

Directions

Give each player a beanbag to balance on the shoulder. On signal, instruct all players to walk with their "heads up" (i.e. not looking down) within the playing area without letting the beanbag fall off. When that occurs tell players to let it drop to the floor. Allow people to resume play when someone else retrieves the beanbag and puts it back in place (while trying to maintain the position of one's own beanbag). Score the game by monitoring the maximum length of time that all players have the beanbag intact. Each time a beanbag falls begin monitoring time again.

Alternative: For additional challenge, require players to move in other ways while balancing the beanbags (i.e. have everyone travel sideways or gallop).

(50) SQUARE SOCCER

Description

Goals: Use kicking and trapping in game situation.

Alignment: Standing spread out on four sides of a square.

Movements: Catching, deflecting, kicking, trapping.

Equipment: One nerf soccer ball for every five people.

Social   Competitive.
   structure: 12-30 players, ages 5 to 8.

Directions

Have Team X occupy Sides 1 and 2 of a square, and Team Y occupy Sides 3 and 4, or have four teams each occupy one side (see Diagram 6.1). Instruct players to kick balls past opponents' endlines while preventing balls from passing their own endlines. Award a point to the kicking team for each ball that goes beyond an endline below the knees. Allow players to trap or block balls with any body parts except hands and arms. Require teams to remain on or behind their kicking lines. With older players allow use of the hands for practicing goalie skills.

Diagram 6.1

Square Soccer

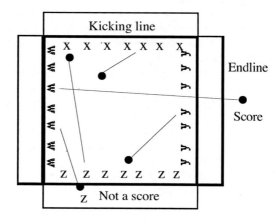

(51) RHYTHMICAL RED LIGHT

Description

Goals:	Respect and trust partner.
	Move at different tempos.
	Stop quickly under control.
	Understand possible outcomes of taking a risk.
Alignment:	Standing with partner inside hoop at one end of area.
Movements:	Balancing, choice of locomotion.
Equipment:	Drum and beater, one hoop for every two players, four markers to indicate scoring lines.
Social structure:	Cooperative within competitive.
	10-30 players, ages 5 to 9.

Directions

Have partners stand inside the hoop while holding it waist high. Designate a drummer to select a form of locomotion and to stand on the midline with her back to the group. Have the drummer hit the drum at whatever constant tempo she chooses. Challenge partners to advance at that tempo as far as possible before the drum stops. The drummer signals to stop with a loud drumbeat, then turns around quickly to see if players are still moving their feet (other body parts may move). Require anyone caught moving to start over. Have the drummer vary the form of locomotion and tempo of the drum in successive rounds. Suggest that the drummer also progress down the floor to remain ahead of all partners (indicated by arrow in Diagram 6.2). Award partners one point for getting to the "midline," and two points for getting to the endline. Give other players a turn playing the drum as time permits.

Note: An adult leader needs to serve as the drummer with children ages 5 to 7.

Alternative: If hoops are not available partners may link elbows instead.

Diagram 6.2
Rhythmical Red Light

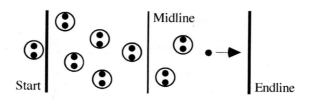

(52) RAINDROPS

Description

Goals: Communicate with others.
                Practice striking one-handed.

Alignment: Standing in a mass at close range.

Movements: Striking one-handed.

Equipment: One 10- to 12-inch balloon per person.

Social   Cooperative.
  structure: 8-30 players, ages 5 to 9.

Directions

Instruct all players to strike their balloons, or "raindrops" vertically into the air. Then have players strike other balloons into the air without hitting the same balloon twice in succession. Require players to leave balloons on the floor once they land. End the game when there are half as many balloons remaining in the air as there are people.

Alternatives: For additional challenge, prevent players from hitting the same color balloon twice in succession. For still more challenge, prevent players from using their hands to strike the balloons after the initial vertical hit.

(53) TOPSY TURVY

Description

Goals: Enhance agility.
                Exercise total body intermittently.

Alignment: Standing scattered on basketball court.

Movements: Bending, dodging, running.

Equipment: Four cones for every five players up to 20, three cones for
                every five players beyond 20.

Social   Competitive.
  structure: 10-40 or more players, ages 5 and up.

Directions

Space cones randomly throughout playing area. Divide players into two groups. Designate one group as "topsys" and the other group as "turvys." Spread out both groups. On signal, have topsys knock down cones continuously until time expires (one or two minutes). Turvys try to concurrently set cones back up as they are able. No topsy or turvy may touch the same cone twice in succession. Score the game by the number of cones tipped over by the topsys when time expires. Have teams change roles and play as many rounds as desired with each round the same length of time.

Note: Tell players to tip over and tip up cones in their original locations using hands only, rather than kicking or bumping them abruptly. Placing cones on individual polydots will help primary level children to keep them spread out.

Alternatives: To create a higher level of activity, require players to alternate sides of the playing area as they tip cones up or over, respectively. For additional challenge, have players travel using a variety of locomotor forms.

(54) AROUND THE HORN

Description

Goals: Practice kicking, throwing, and catching.
Understand need to pass ball quickly, yet accurately.

Alignment: Half the players spread out in field; half the players lined up to kick.

Movements: Batting, catching, kicking, punting, running, throwing overhand.

Equipment: Kickball, four bases.

Social structure: Cooperative within competitive.
16-24 players, ages 7 to 10.

Directions

Kickers: Divide kickers into two even groups. Have groups count off 1-4 and 11-14, respectively to determine kicking order (with eight kickers at a time). Line up both groups behind the endline, with the group numbered 1-4 in front of the group numbered 11-14, as shown in Diagram 6.3. Have Player 1 kick a rolled ball from the pitcher into fair territory. If the player does not kick a fair ball, require him to kick a stationary ball resting at home plate. Following the fair kick, instruct all players in that group to run in order around the bases as far as possible (indicated by dotted arrows in the figure). Score one run for each player who reaches third base. Then Player 11 kicks and that group follows him around the bases. Allow half the players on a team to kick before switching to the field (i.e. players 1, 11, 2, 12).

Fielders: Have players retrieve the kicked ball and return it to the pitcher to stop the runners' scoring. Require fielders to advance the ball by passing it to four different teammates (six teammates with 20-24 players). Have the last pass go to the pitcher. One possible passing sequence is indicated by numbers in Diagram 6.3. Do not count the player who retrieves the ball as one of the passes, and do not allow players to travel while holding the ball. Following each kick, rotate fielding positions in the order indicated by letters a through g in the diagram.

Alternative: To increase scoring, eliminate second base.

Diagram 6.3

Around the Horn

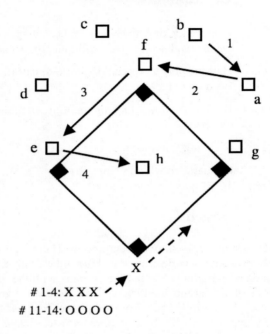

1-4: X X X
11-14: O O O O

(55) DOT BALL

Description

Goals: Practice throwing and catching.
                  Understand need to pass ball quickly, yet accurately.
                  Practice agility running.

Alignment: Striking team standing in three lines behind the endline
                  of basketball court; fielding team standing on polydots
                  scattered behind the midline of the court.

Movements: Catching, running, striking one-handed, throwing
                  overhand, tossing underhand.

Equipment: Soft, pliable ball, enough polydots for one team.

Social   Cooperative within competitive.
   structure: 15-30 players, ages 7 to 11.

Directions

Striking team: Have the first person in the middle line strike the ball out of her hand so it crosses the quarterline. Tell the first runner in the other two lines to run around the nearest marker and back across the endline. If a marker is knocked down or misplaced, require the runner to replace it. Have runners continue rounding their markers in order, earning a point each time, until the fielding team completes their tasks. Tell runners they may run more than one time. Have each player in the middle line strike the ball before switching to the field.

Fielding team: While the batting team rounds markers, instruct the fielding team to complete six throws and catches without dropping the ball. The sequence of catches numbered in Diagram 6.4 indicates an extra throw because one was dropped (dotted line). Do not allow the same player to receive the ball twice during the same turn. Require players to have at least one foot on their dots to throw or catch the ball. After fielders complete passes, tell them to change to a different dot for the next turn. Blow a whistle when fielders have changed dots to end the strikers' scoring for that turn. Have runners in process become the first runner for the next turn. As time permits, rotate players to the striking line for future innings.

Diagram 6.4
Dot Ball

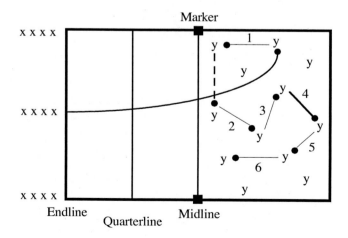

(56) BLOCKADE

Description

Goals: Practice kicking and trapping in game situation.

Alignment: Two teams lined up on opposite sides of a rectangle; one team spread out in middle.

Movements: Kicking, trapping.

Equipment: One nerf soccer ball for every four players, polydots to outline center rectangle.

Social   Competitive.
  structure: 15-24 players, ages 7 to 11.

Directions

Form three small groups of five to eight players. Spread out two teams on the sides of a basketball court. Spread out the third team as a "blockade" in the middle (Team <u>B</u> in Diagram 6.5). Instruct sideline players to kick balls back and forth on the floor to avoid the blockade. When blockade players intercept a ball, instruct them to kick it back to the same side. Award one point to both sideline teams for each trap of a ball kicked on the floor through the blockade. Rotate other teams to the middle in three-minute intervals. Following each round, total up individual points and award the total to each sideline team.

Diagram 6.5

Blockade

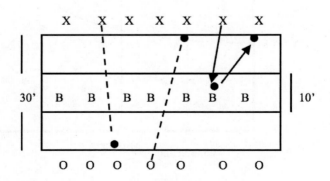

(57) SCOOTER BALL

Description

Goals: Exercise total body intermittently.
Practice throwing and catching in game situation.
Understand value of moving without ball to open areas.

Alignment: Half the players standing on endlines; half the players sitting on scooters in the middle.

Movements: Catching, deflecting, scooting, throwing.

Equipment: One scooter and pinney for half the players, one foam ball for every eight people.

Social
structure: Competitive.
16-32 players, ages 7 to 12.

Directions

Divide players into two teams and have one team wear pinnies. Within each team, have half the players stand on their endline as goalies and half the players sit on a scooter in the middle (see Diagram 6.6). Spread out middle players by restricting them to designated halves of the playing area (halfbacks and forwards, respectively).

Begin by giving goalies on each endline an equal number of balls. Goalies may pass balls to halfbacks only, and halfbacks pass balls to forwards only. Halfbacks and forwards may only move on their scooters *without* the ball. Forwards try to score by throwing balls past goalies below the shoulders. One point is scored offensively for each goal, and one point is scored defensively each time a goalie catches a ball on a fly. Encourage players to monitor individual scoring and add scores together at stoppage of play. Whether or not a point is scored, goalies put all balls that reach an endline back in play by throwing them to a respective halfback.

Diagram 6.6

Scooter Ball

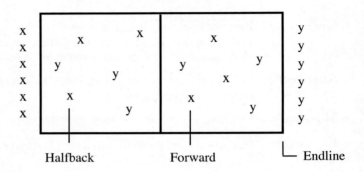

Halfback   Forward   ⌐ Endline

(58) EVERYBODY IT

Description

Goals: Exercise total body intermittently.
                 Move in relation to others safely.

Alignment: Standing scattered on basketball or volleyball court,
                 depending on number of players.

Movements: Dodging, running, shuffling, tagging.

Equipment: Markers to outline area.

Social   Competitive.
   structure: 8-40 or more players, ages 7 and up.

Directions

On signal, tell all players to tag one another. Have tagged players sit down where they are tagged, but continue tagging. Require sitting players to cross their legs and maintain an upright posture to avoid being stepped on or tripping others. If players tag one another simultaneously, or are unsure who tagged first, have both players sit down. Players who step outside the boundaries sit down at the place they crossed the line.

Alternative: For additional challenge, require standing players to tag with their nondominant hands only.

(59) COLOR TAG

Description

Goals: Exercise total body intermittently.
                 Practice dodging.
                 Move in relation to others safely.

Alignment: Two teams spread out on edge of rectangular playing
                 area; one team in center circle.

Movements: Dodging, running, tagging.

Equipment: Pinnies of three different colors, markers to outline area,
                 polydots to form center circle, stopwatch.

Social   Competitive.
structure: 15-40 or more players (if outdoors or in large gym), ages
                 7 and up.

Directions

Group players into three teams and disperse pinnies of three colors to distinguish teams. Spread out one team in the center circle as "dodgers," and two teams on the perimeter as "taggers." On signal, dodgers may travel anywhere inside the boundaries of a basketball court (15-20 players) or small soccer field (21-40 players). Taggers try to tag dodgers as soon as possible. As dodgers are tagged, they stand outside the boundaries taking the shortest possible route. The length of time it takes for all the dodgers to be tagged becomes that team's score (lower number is better). Rotate players so each team has two turns as dodgers.

(60) FLAG TAG

Description

Goals:	Exercise total body continuously. Practice dodging. Move in relation to others safely.
Alignment:	Standing scattered on basketball or volleyball court, depending on number of players.
Movements:	Dodging, grasping, running, tagging.
Equipment:	Markers to outline area, one nylon belt with two flags per person.
Social structure:	Competitive. 8-40 or more players (if outdoors or in large gym), ages 7 and up.

Directions

Give all players a belt with two flags to wear so flags can be easily seen (not covered with hand or clothing). On signal, tell all players to grasp flags from the belts of other players. Have players who leave the boundaries give a flag to the nearest player. When a player loses both flags, allow him to remain in the game to grasp other flags. Stop the game while several players still have at least one flag. Award one point for each flag grasped from opponent's belts, and two points for each flag remaining on a person's belt.

Alternative: For variety, play the game with two to four teams using different colored flags.

(61) FLAG CHASERS

Description

Goals: Exercise total body continuously.
                Practice dodging.
                Move in relation to others safely.

Alignment: Standing scattered on basketball or volleyball court,
                depending on number of players.

Movements: Dodging, grasping, running.

Equipment: Markers to outline area, one nylon belt with one flag per
                per person, one base for every five people.

Social   Competitive.
  Structure: 8-40 or more players (if outdoors or in large gym), ages 7
                and up.

Directions

Flag Chasers has similar characteristics to *Flag Tag* (p. 112), but also
important distinguishing features. Give all players a belt with one flag to
wear so it can be easily seen (not covered with hand or clothing). Spread
out bases throughout the area. Remove the flag from one sixth of the
players and designate them as initial chasers. On signal, instruct the
chasers to grasp a flag from any runner. When that occurs, the chaser and
runner exchange roles and the former chaser wears the flag. (The only
chasers are the group of players without a flag at any given time.) If a
flag falls to the floor, any player without a flag may pick it up and wear it.

Utilize bases as safety spots. Any runner may occupy a base until another
runner arrives. The most recent runner to arrive always wins possession
of a base. Once a player leaves a base she cannot return until occupying
another base. If two players are uncertain about who arrived at a base last
they both leave and cannot return until occupying a different base.
Players may keep track of how many times they lose a flag, not counting
the initial chasers (fewer is better).

(62) SCATTER DODGEBALL

Description

Goals: Practice throwing two-handed.
                    Exercise total body intermittently.
                    Understand possible outcomes of taking a risk.

Alignment: Standing on perimeter of basketball or volleyball court.

Movements: Catching, dodging, running, throwing two-handed.

Equipment: One 6- to 8-inch playground or plastic ball for every six
                    people, markers to outline area.

Social   Competitive.
   structure: 8-40 or more players (if outdoors or in large gym), ages 7
                    and up.

Directions

Place the balls in the middle of the playing area. On signal, instruct most players to scatter, while those who wish may dart for a ball. Tell players with balls to hit others below the shoulders using a two-hand throw. Do not allow players who initially retrieve a ball to hit each other. Allow players to have only one ball at a time, and to take only one step while holding a ball (unlimited steps without ball). When someone is hit on a fly, or when a person's throw is caught on a fly, he sits down with legs crossed in that location. Allow players to stand up again under two conditions:

1. When the player who hit her sits down (if known).
2. When a stray ball comes within reach (while still sitting).

Score the game by the number of players each individual hits, or by which players are standing when time expires.

Alternative: For variety, scatter two to four teams throughout the area, having each team try to hit the other team's players (wearing different colored pinnies). For additional challenge utilize foam balls and allow throwing with one hand.

(63) MAT BALL

Description

Goals: Practice throwing and catching.
Understand value of moving without ball.
Practice dodging and guarding.

Alignment: Standing spread out on basketball court.

Movements: Catching, dodging, guarding, throwing one- and two-handed.

Equipment: One 6- to 8-inch foam ball for every five people with different colors for each team, four mats, polydots to outline mats, pinnies for one team.

Social
structure: Competitive.
16-32 players, ages 8 to 12.

Directions

Divide players into two teams and have one team wear pinnies. Designate two players from each team as "receivers," and position them on mats as indicated in Diagram 6.7. Spread out remaining players equally on the two halves of the court (or larger area for 24-32 people). Give receivers at one end of the court each two balls of different colors. On signal, instruct them to pass balls to teammates, eventually trying to complete passes to their team's diagonal mat (one sequence depicted in figure by dotted arrows). Teams score one point for each completion to a receiver provided that:

1. Receivers have both feet on the mat when catching ball.
2. No pass is thrown from a mat across the midline, or from one side of the midline to a far mat.
3. All players remain on their designated sides.

Whenever points are scored, or receivers retrieve a ball in the polydot area, they pass the ball to attempt to score the other direction. No other player may enter the polydot area (indicated by dotted lines). Rotate players to mats periodically.

Diagram 6.7
Mat Ball

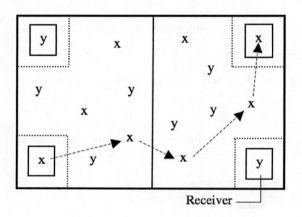

Receiver

Diagram 6.8
Pin Soccer

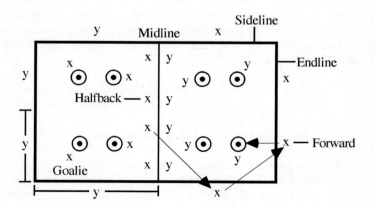

(64) PIN SOCCER

Description

Goals:	Use kicking and trapping in game situation. Practice kicking and passing accuracy. Understand value of passing in order to score.
Alignment:	Standing on two sides of playing area in three designated groups.
Movements:	Guarding, kicking, passing, trapping.
Equipment:	One youth soccer ball for every four people, six or eight pins, two different colored jerseys (one per person).
Social structure:	Competitive. 12-24 players, ages 8 to 12.

Directions

To the extent possible, divide players into three equal groups within each team. Have goalies stand near the pins, halfbacks stand near the midline on their defensive side, and forwards stand around the perimeter on their offensive side. Require goalies to remain outside the tires surrounding the pins, and forwards to remain between the slash marks shown in Diagram 6.8. Have halfbacks begin with the balls.

On signal, instruct halfbacks and forwards to knock down pins of the opponent with accurate kicking. Award one point for each pin that falls, even if the opponent knocks one over accidentally. Each time a pin falls tell that team to reset it immediately so it may be knocked down again. Scoring is more likely when players pass the ball, as illustrated in the diagram with arrows. At the end of each five-minute period, combine player's individual points and rotate them to new positions within their teams. Switch goalies to halfbacks, halfbacks to forwards and forwards to goalies.

(65) GARBAGE BALL

Description

Goals:	Practice throwing overhand and catching.
	Practice guarding opponent.
	Understand value of passing in order to score.
Alignment:	Each of four teams standing on their respective sides of a square, facing the center; Player 1 from each line standing in the scoring zone opposite her line, holding a ball; Player 2 standing in the defensive zone to her left.
Movements:	Catching, guarding, throwing overhand.
Equipment:	Eight 6-inch foam or rubber balls, large garbage can, four different colored pinnies.
Social structure:	Competitive.
	20-32 players, ages 8 to 12.

Directions

Give each player in a scoring zone a ball. Tell her to make as many baskets as possible in a given round. Require players to catch a ball thrown from their team's endline on a fly, before attempting a basket with that same ball (indicated for Player w1 in Diagram 6.9). Have a player who acquires a ball in any other manner also first throw it to her endline so it may be thrown to the scoring zone. Encourage players in the defensive and scoring zones to intercept an opponent's pass, as long as they remain in their respective zones.

When a basket is made, leave the ball in the garbage can until the end of the round. Each time a ball lands in the garbage can, throw in a new ball to the player that made the basket (until all 10 balls have entered game). End a round when eight baskets have been made. Following each round, rotate players clockwise.

Diagram 6.9
Garbage Ball

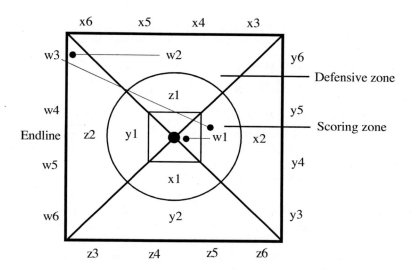

Diagram 6.10
Sideline Basketball

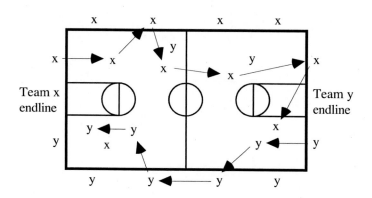

(66) SIDELINE BASKETBALL

Description

Goals: Practice basketball skills in game situation.
Exercise total body intermittently.
Understand value of passing in order to score.

Alignment: 8-14 players standing on sideline; 6-10 players on court.

Movements: Guarding, passing, shooting.

Equipment: Two youth basketballs.

Social   Cooperative within competitive.
structure: 14-24 players, ages 8 to 12.

Directions

Give each team a basketball behind its own endline. Instruct teams to advance the ball up the court to score while at the same time trying to prevent the other team from scoring. Allow the ball to be advanced by passing only. Permit the ball to be passed to sideline and endline players, but not three times consecutively (refer to Diagram 6.10). Require sideline and endline players to remain behind their lines. Keep play continuous by (a) having the closest sideline player immediately inbound a ball that leaves the boundaries, and (b) having the opposite endline player immediately inbound a ball following a basket. Following traveling and other violations, give the ball to the other team's closest sideline player. Rotate different sideline and endline players onto the court every five minutes.

(67) BEACH BALL BLAST

Description

Goals: Practice throwing overhand in game situation.
              Exercise total body intermittently.

Alignment: Half the players standing on each end of volleyball court.

Movements: Collecting, throwing overhand.

Equipment: Large beach ball (48" or more), one yarn ball or small
              gator ball per person.

Social   Competitive or cooperative.
  structure: 16-32 players, ages 8 to 12.

Directions

Line up players on their respective endlines and give each person a ball. Position the beach ball on the centerline. On signal, instruct players to throw the yarn balls at the beach ball, trying to make it roll across the opposite endline. After the initial throw, have players repeatedly retrieve a ball and throw it quickly. Teams may advance as far as their 10-foot lines once play begins. They may advance as far as the centerline once the ball passes the opponent's 10-foot line. If any player touches the beach ball at any time, award a victory to the other team and begin a new round.

Note: Even though volleyball lines are used as restraining lines fore and aft, the width of the playing area may extend as far as the facility permits.

Alternatives: For variety, divide players into four teams and align them in a square. Have each team try to prevent the beach ball from crossing its endline. With fewer than 16 players challenge the group to work cooperatively to move the beach ball to a specified location or through a specified path on the floor.

(68) HUDDLE UP

Description

Goals: Respect others.
                   Utilize reaction time in game situation.
                   Practice forming groups quickly.

Alignment: Standing scattered within basketball court.

Movements: Huddling, variety of forms of locomotion.

Equipment: One jump rope for every two players.

Social   Competitive and cooperative.
   structure: 16-40 or more players, ages 8 to 14.

Directions

Spread out players throughout the basketball court. Spread out jump ropes outside the court. On signal, instruct players to jog in all directions wherever there is open space. After a short while, call out any designated size of groupings desired between two and five (by simply yelling "fives"). Groups may be as large as six or seven with more than 30 players. Players are to quickly huddle up in that size of groupings. Whoever fails to get in a huddle the correct size leaves the boundaries and jumps rope 20 times while the leader continues calling groupings for remaining players (intermittently jogging and huddling up). After jumping rope, players may re-enter the game at a "gate" near the leader so the leader can carefully time re-entry during a jogging segment, rather than during a huddling segment. Method and direction of traveling may be changed at will. Have players keep track of the number of times they exit the game (fewer is better).

(69) CHAIN TAG

Description

Goals: Respect and trust others.
Exercise total body continuously.
Practice dodging.

Alignment: Standing with chains equally spaced on perimeter of rectangle or square, facing center of area.

Movements: Dodging, running, tagging.

Equipment: Hoop (if center circle is not available), markers to outline area.

Social
structure: Cooperative within competitive.
3-5 players per chain (3-6 chains), ages 8 and up.

Directions

Designate a tagger to stand in the center circle, and arrange chains in the manner depicted by Line a in Diagram 6.11. On signal, allow chains to move anywhere in the boundaries, without separating and without forming a closed chain or circle. Allow any other shape in order to protect ends of chains. Possible shapes are depicted by Lines b, c and d in the diagram. Have the tagger try to tag an end person of any chain and return to the circle. Then have the tagger try to repeat this procedure as often as possible in 60 seconds (by tagging the same player or different ends of chains). Award the tagger one point for each time (a) an end person is tagged, (b) a chain comes apart, or (c) a chain steps out of bounds (any one of its players). Appoint several players to be tagger as time permits. Each time taggers switch, rotate different players to the ends of chains.

Note: The younger the players, the shorter the chains need to be.

Alternatives: Extend the time limit to 90 seconds to encourage more exercise and more scoring. In addition, appoint two taggers at a time with five or six chains in the game.

Diagram 6.11
Chain Tag

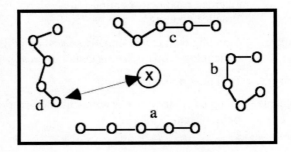

Diagram 6.12
Dribble Tag

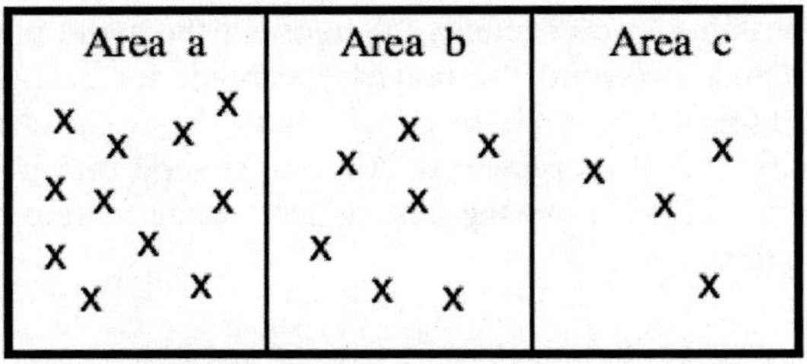

Area a	Area b	Area c

x x x x
x x   x
x   x
  x   x
	x x
	x x
	   x
	x
	  x x
		x
		x x
		    x
		    x

(70) DRIBBLE TAG

Description

Goals:	Practice positioning body. Practice dribbling. Understand trade-off between protecting own ball and attacking other balls.
Alignment:	Standing scattered inside one-third of basketball court.
Movements:	Dodging, dribbling.
Equipment:	Markers to divide area into three sections, one youth soccer ball per person.
Social structure:	Competitive. 8-30 players, ages 8 and up.

Directions

On signal, instruct players to dribble a ball in one-third of the court, labeled Area a̱ in Diagram 6.12. At the same time, challenge players to kick other balls outside that area. Have anyone whose ball leaves Area a̱, retrieve it and enter Area ḇ. If a player's ball is kicked out of Area ḇ, have that player enter a third game in Area c̱. If a player's ball is kicked out of Area c̱, tell him to retrieve it and continue playing in that area. Begin another round when only one player remains in Area a̱. If necessary, reduce the size of Area a̱ when only a few players remain.

Alternative: For variety, play the game dribbling with hands, instead of with feet, substituting a youth basketball for the soccer ball. In this case, advance a player to the next area if he loses control of the dribble, even if the ball does not leave the area.

(71) LINK BALL

Description

Goals:	Respect and trust others.
	Practice throwing and catching.
	Practice dodging.
Alignment:	Standing scattered equally on each half of area.
Movements:	Catching, dodging, throwing one-handed.
Equipment:	One 8-inch nerf or gator ball for every four people, markers to designate midline and outside boundaries.
Social structure:	Cooperative within competitive. 15-30 players, ages 9 to 14.

Directions

Instruct players to hit opponents using a one-hand throw. Have a player who is hit on a fly, or whose throw is caught on a fly, become a shagger in her end zone. Tell shaggers to retrieve loose balls and toss them to teammates without leaving the end zone, as shown in Diagram 6.13. When a second player enters the same end zone, have teammates link elbows together and return to their original side (likewise with the third and fourth players).

Have linked players continue throwing and catching balls using their outside arms, but allow them to travel anywhere in the playing area, even across the midline. When one of the linked players is hit by a fly ball, or throws a ball that is caught, require that pair to return to the end zone to get different partners. No more than two people will remain in the end zone at a given time. One team wins when all players from the other team are either linked or in their end zone.

Note: Have all players enter and leave end zones along the perimeter of the playing area.

Figure 6.2: Illustration of *Link Ball*.

Diagram 6.13
Link Ball

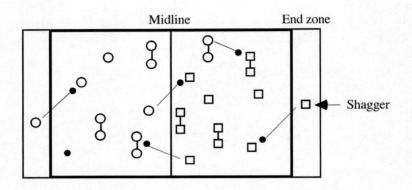

Diagram 6.14
Quadrant Ball

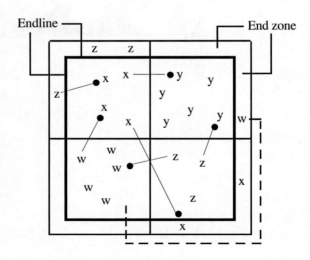

(72) QUADRANT BALL

Description

Goals:	Practice throwing and catching.
	Use peripheral vision.
	Understand value of passing in order to score.
Alignment:	Each group standing on its endline.
Movements:	Catching, dodging, throwing one-handed.
Equipment:	Markers to outline four squares and end zones, one 8-inch nerf ball for every four players, pinnies of four different colors (one per person).
Social structure:	Competitive.
	16-32 players, ages 9 to 14.

Directions

Have players get balls from the middle of each square and try to hit people on other teams. Limit players to one ball at a time, and one step while holding a ball (unlimited steps without ball). When someone is hit on a fly, or when a throw is caught on a fly, have that player go to the end zone diagonally opposite his square without cutting through another square (see dotted line in Diagram 6.14). Encourage end zone players to continue throwing at opponents as they acquire stray balls, depicted by Team Z in the diagram. If an end zone player catches a ball on a fly (usually from teammate), have the player return to his square without cutting through other squares.

Allow end zone players to retrieve balls that leave the back of the end zone, providing they return before throwing the ball. Challenge teams to have the most people in their squares when time expires. When time expires, have players complete transitions to and from end zones before counting points.

(73) CABOOSE BALL

Description

Goals: Practice throwing and dodging in game situation.
                 Improve body awareness.
                 Cooperate with, and respect others.

Alignment: Standing on perimeter of circle with designated groups in
                 the center.

Movements: Dodging and throwing overhand.

Equipment: Two or three 8-1/2-inch foam balls and polydots to mark
                 circle if necessary.

Social   Competitive and cooperative.
    structure: 3-5 players per group, 4-5 groups, ages 9 to 14.

Directions

Divide players into small groups, the younger the players, the smaller the
groups. Have two groups line up in the middle of a large circle in a
separate "train" front-to-back by holding onto each other's waists.
Spread out remaining players on the circle. Disperse two or three balls to
different players on the circle. Instruct circle players to throw balls at the
back player, or "caboose," of each train. Recommend that circle players
pass balls rapidly to each other to get the best shot at a caboose. When a
caboose is hit, have that player quickly rotate to the front of the train and
continue play. Rotate new groups to the middle every two or three
minutes. Score the game by the number of times each train has its
caboose hit (fewer is better).

Trains are free to maneuver in any manner to avoid balls, as long as they
do not (a) come apart, or (b) close their shape into a complete circle.
Each time one of the errors occurs, give another point to that respective
train.

(74) ORBIT

Description

Goals: Respect other people's spaces.
Practice reacting to ball quickly.

Alignment: Half the players resting on their backs in a circle facing away from the center; half the players standing outside the circle facing the center.

Movements: Balancing, kicking two-footed, pushing.

Equipment: 36- or 48-inch cage ball, one polydot for every two people.

Social
structure: Competitive.
12-20 players, ages 10 to 14.

Directions

Stand half the players on a circle (or on a circle of individual polydots). Rest half the players on their backs, lifting feet off the floor. Toss the ball toward the feet of the resting players. Award resting players a point every time they kick the ball "into orbit" outside the circle of standing players, as indicated in Diagram 6.15. Challenge standing players to restrain the ball while keeping at least one foot on their circle or dots. Award standing players a point every time the ball touches the floor inside the circle of resting players. When the ball lands on the floor in the neutral zone, have the nearest standing player toss it back into play. Make the neutral zone and inner circle smaller or larger to allow more or less scoring, respectively. Reverse roles of teams every five minutes.

Note: Have resting players remove eyeglasses and keep their heads on the floor to avoid possible injury.

Diagram 6.15
Orbit

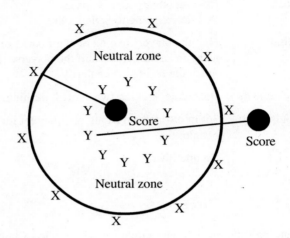

Diagram 6.16

Double Trouble

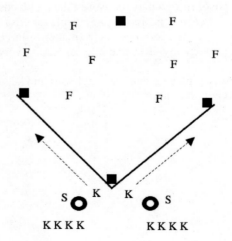

(75) DOUBLE TROUBLE

Description

Goals: Practice kicking, passing and trapping.
                  Understand need to pass balls quickly, yet accurately.
                  Practice reacting to ball quickly.

Alignment: Half the players up to bat; half the players spread out in
                  the field beyond the midline.

Movements: Kicking, passing, running, trapping.

Equipment: Two playground balls and bicycle tires.

Social   Cooperative within competitive.
  structure: 16-24 players, ages 10 to 14.

Directions

Kickers (designated K in Diagram 6.16): Have two people each take a
ball from a tire and rest it on the floor next to the tire. Instruct kickers to
kick balls simultaneously and begin running opposite directions around
bases. All successful contacts of the ball are considered "fair balls."
Kickers score one point for completing each cycle, or four bases, before
balls are "stabilized."

Fielders (designated F in Diagram 6.16): Have fielders designate two
"stabilizers" (indicated S in Diagram). One stabilizer is positioned
outside each tire out of the way of kickers. After balls are kicked, fielders
pass them with the feet to one another and then to a stabilizer, who
returns them with the feet to a resting position inside the respective tires.
A ball must be passed at least two times before passing it to a stabilizer to
position it in a tire.

Alternatives: If scoring is too difficult, shorten the bases or eliminate a
base.

(76) BIG BASE

Description

Goals: Respect other people's spaces.
                Practice reacting to ball quickly.
                Understand value of passing balls in order to hit
                opponents.

Alignment: Half the players up to bat; half the players spread out in
                the field outside the neutral zone.

Movements: Catching, kicking, running, throwing.

Equipment: Two playground balls, four mats as bases.

Social   Cooperative within competitive.
  structure: 16-32 players, ages 10 to 14.

Directions

Kickers (designated K̲ in Diagram 6.17): Have two people each kick a
rolled ball from their respective pitchers (indicated by dotted arrows). All
successful contacts of the ball are considered "fair balls." Kickers begin
running around bases indicated with large folding mats. Runners score
one point for reaching the 4th base. Runners may stop on a base at any
time, or may choose not to run on a teammate's kick (multiple runners
may occupy a base). However, a runner must advance at least one base
after stepping off a base. Have all players kick before switching to the
field, rather than recording outs.

Fielders (designated F̲ in Diagram 6.17): Have fielders pass balls to one
another until they can be (a) thrown at a runner, or (b) caught by a pitcher
on a pitching spot. Either ball may be thrown at either runner. Fielders
may not travel while holding a ball, but are encouraged to take a step
while throwing. A traveling violation results in an additional point for
the kicking team. Once both balls are returned to the pitchers, runners
must remain on a base, or return to the previous base if already part way.

Alternatives: Twelve to 14-year-olds could be allowed to steal bases, and
to complete multiple cycles of the bases at their own risk. (i.e. If a runner
gets thrown out after completing a cycle, previous points that turn are
forfeited.) For variety, substitute batting for kicking. In this case, have

players choose to bat a pitched ball or toss the ball to themselves. Also allow players to choose from two different sizes of bats and balls.

Diagram 6.17

Big Base

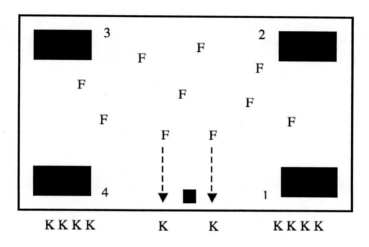

(77) FRISBEE FRAME

Description

Goals:	Practice throwing and catching. Understand type of throw needed to hit open area.
Alignment:	Standing scattered in each of four squares.
Movements:	Catching, throwing one-handed.
Equipment:	One Frisbee or disc for every four players, 16 bicycle tires, markers to outline area.
Social structure:	Competitive. 16-32 players, ages 10 and up.

Directions

Disperse discs equally throughout quadrants. On signal, instruct players to throw discs into other quadrants so they touch the ground before being caught (indicated by arrows in Diagram 6.18). Allow discs to be caught anywhere within a given team's quadrant, but require them to be thrown from within one of the team's bicycle tires. Have the closest team retrieve discs that land out of bounds, but return to the playing area before throwing them again. Award one point for each successful throw and one point for each fly caught. Subtract one point for each errant throw (that lands short or out of bounds) and for each fly missed (touched on a fly but dropped). Have each player monitor individual points and add them to the team total.

Diagram 6.18

Frisbee Frame

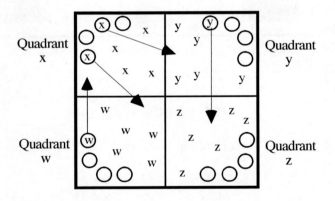

Chapter 7

Relay Games

R elays may or may not be considered games, depending on the breadth of the definition used. Relays are included here because a broad definition of games is used, and because leaders are attracted to the simple structure and easy preparation required. In addition, most children and adolescents participate in relays enthusiastically. Although relays have these advantages, traditional ones are potentially harmful to players. Traditional relays are defined as those that are common; activities that are taught by leaders simply because the leaders experienced those activities when they were young. The same question needs to be posed of a relay as with any other game: Can players of all abilities succeed? At least four problems may prevent players from succeeding in traditional relays, though perhaps not all problems hold true for all relays. Each problem is explained below along with ways to alleviate the problem.

Amount of Activity

One problem with traditional relays involves too many people standing in line waiting for a turn. Consequently, any given player gets minimal activity. Williams (1992) estimates the amount of activity to be 6% of the total time allocated to relay activities when considering the administrative time required for determining teams, setting up equipment, explaining procedures, and transitioning between tasks. An indirect result of standing in line too long is that the lack of engagement contributes to misbehavior. Players tend to fill their time doing something, even if that something is counterproductive. Unless administrative time can be significantly reduced, and activity time significantly increased, William's admonition to eliminate relays altogether is warranted.

The problem of group size may be addressed by simply having smaller groups. Figure 7.1 indicates two ways to divide 24 people into teams of three, rather than six, players. One modification involves spreading out eight teams the other direction in the gym (facing the width, rather than the length, of the court). The other modification requires having four groups on each end of the court facing one another. In this scenario, players turn around in the middle, rather than moving to the end of the court. Naturally, a neutral zone is needed in the middle so players from opposite ends do not collide with one another. In addition, activities cannot involve manipulating equipment so that objects are out of control beyond the neutral zone. Given this concern, activities with balloons are particularly suitable (see pp. 143-145). With either scenario in Figure 7.1, having players travel a shorter distance ends a given relay sooner, allowing the teacher to interject comments at more frequent intervals. Traveling shorter distances also gives leaders the option to use relays for a smaller percentage of the total instructional time.

If class size dictates that teams need to have more than three players, then two or three players per group can be active at a time. Two participants can be active anytime activities require partners to cooperate. In the *Balloon Trapping* relay (p. 144) partners trap a filled balloon between their bodies. Three players per team can be active by having the second and third people in line perform a callisthenic while the first person completes the relay. The organization in Figure 7.2 numbers players 1 through 6, with enough room for three players per team to be active at any given time. One relay that utilizes this organization is built around the theme of a special event (see *Mountain Triathlon*, p. 150). Other themes for relays could include holidays or seasons of the year.

Occasionally, the intensity of activity involved in a relay is great enough to warrant having teams with four to six players, even when only one is active at a time. In such cases, the inactive time provides an intentional rest so players can complete the task several times. *Give 'n Take* (p. 152) and *Lap Tag* (p. 160) are examples of repetitive relays involving running at a high intensity level.

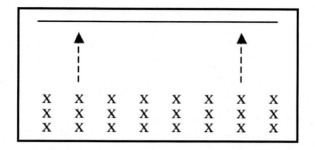

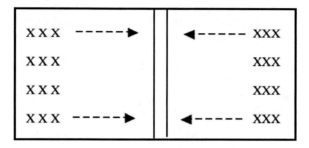

Figure 7.1

Arranging Three Players Per Team

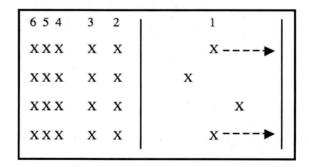

Figure 7.2

Involving Multiple Players Per Team

Quality of Skill

A second problem with relays is their tendency to foster poor quality skill practice. So much emphasis is placed on winning that children's desire for speed overcomes any motivation to perform a skill well (Pangrazi, 2001; Schwager, 1992). Common examples include dribbling a basketball shoulder height, or kicking a soccer ball and running after it, rather than dribbling it close range with many touches.

One way to address quality of skills in relays is to incorporate basic skills already mastered by players. Forms of locomotion, for instance, may be practiced at a fast speed with no negative side effects. As long as a given locomotor skill is mechanically correct, and the relay is organized safely, it makes no difference whether a child performs the skill with a shorter or longer stride, or in a smooth or jerky manner. Other basic skills or exercises may be incorporated into relays without focusing on speed. In *Mountain Triathlon* (p. 150), for instance, the mountain climber and slalom jump calisthenics are utilized by teammates of those performing the relay activity. No pressure exists to complete a certain number of repetitions.

A second way to address quality of skills is to incorporate common or novel tasks in relays that bear little resemblance to common sport skills. Novel tasks might utilize unusual equipment, or utilize common equipment in unusual ways. A task using unusual equipment might include pushing a beach ball with a wand. A task that uses common equipment in an unusual way might be depicting a swimming stroke while moving on a scooter (again, see *Mountain Triathlon*).

Public Scrutiny

A third drawback of traditional relays is the tendency to place inexperienced performers "in the spotlight" (Belka, 1999; Schwager, 1992; Williams, 1992). When only one performer per line moves at a time, most children are free to watch intently what the others are doing—and worse—how the others are doing. With 24 people involved in a relay, and 6 per line, 18 people stand and watch at any given time. This ratio can be worse toward the end of a relay. If three groups have finished, and one person remains active, then 23 people are watching the final person finish. The stress and lack of esteem associated with public scrutiny can be devastating to players who do not perform well.

Pangrazi (2001) recommends taking lower skilled players out of the spotlight by placing them in the middle of lines. Although this will help to a degree, changing positions of players is difficult to accomplish without "telegraphing" differences in ability. Another possible way to remove players from the spotlight is by using novel activities that help equalize abilities. Peers are less likely to criticize performance when they don't have a common understanding of how a novel task is to be performed. An additional idea concerning the timing of relays improves participation and reduces public scrutiny. Instead of ending a relay when each person has one turn, activity may continue until a specified amount of time expires, or enough time to allow all people two or more turns.

Timing a relay allows more people to remain active because at least one person per line is always on the move, instead of waiting for slower lines to finish. Timing a relay also discourages children from focusing on the performance of players in other lines, because (a) it is more difficult to measure the progress of other teams while all teams remain active, (b) all players potentially need to be ready for another turn, and (c) any given player's own line needs encouragement until activity is stopped.

An indirect benefit of timing relays is that lines do not need to compensate for having different numbers of players. Teams simply get one point for each person that completes the movements. Since all teams are active until time is stopped, each team has equal opportunity to score, even when it has one less player. Any player that is part way through a turn when time stops would be the first participant in the next relay.

Sportsmanship

Poor sportsmanship presents a fourth problem with traditional relays. High structural and intentional competition often encourage poor sportsmanship, both within and between teams. Sportsmanship within teams suffers because activities are individually performed. Activities are not designed for players to help one another. Instead, players are more likely to ridicule or otherwise criticize teammates who jeopardize the performance of the team overall. Sportsmanship between teams suffers because players often feel a need to "officiate" for other teams, rather than simply monitor their own team's performance. Pointing the finger at others and bending rules for personal advantage is normative (Schwager, 1992).

Some modifications suggested above necessarily improve sportsmanship to the degree that they are carried out effectively. Incorporating partner tasks causes players to work together with less individualistic mindsets. Using novel tasks helps peers empathize with other performers because (a) they don't have a common understanding of how to perform a novel task, and (b) they may struggle to complete the task themselves. Timing relays results in less criticism of others. It also reduces structural and intentional competition because the progress of teams is less visible.

Sportsmanship can also be improved, in part, by discussing expectations concerning organizational procedures and virtues of character before starting relays. Organizational features need to be explained (and often demonstrated) in very concrete terms. When players know they are accountable for how they begin, perform and end a relay they are more likely to follow expectations. Virtues particularly critical in relays include honesty and self-control. Honesty is critical because leaders cannot possibly monitor the choices of all participants. Players need to understand that following relay rules is necessary to accomplish the exercise, practice, and fun intended. Self-control can be addressed from the standpoint of noise level and interpersonal communication. Players can have fun and support others without yelling and screaming. They can also learn appropriate ways to express disappointment and/or disagreement if leaders model respectful statements. Several other virtues are discussed in the context of game play in the companion book (Henkel, 2010).

Having discussed problems associated with traditional relays, and ways to alleviate the problems, the rest of chapter 7 outlines 17 specific relay games. Leaders need to select relays that accomplish targeted objectives with an understanding that some relays are more recreational than educational, and vice verse. Whatever relays are chosen, they are not appropriate for preschool and early childhood programs (Belka, 1999). Instead, the same general guideline could be applied as with age of onset for organized sports, namely, about age eight or third grade (see discussion on pp. 33-34). Relays in this chapter begin at age seven due to the carefully selected content and parameters in general.

(78) BALLOON BATTING

Description

Goals: Practice striking.
Utilize eye-hand coordination.
Understand how to use force to make an object go specific directions.

Alignment: Sitting in lines all facing the same direction.

Movements: One- or two-hand striking, running, walking.

Equipment: One 10- to 12-inch balloon per group with extra balloons available, two cones per group.

Social
structure: Competitive and cooperative.
3-4 people per group, ages 7 to 12.

Directions

Give the first person in each line (Player 1) a balloon. On signal, instruct Players 1 and 2 to stand and alternate striking or batting the balloon forward while moving down around the cone and back again. Batting the balloon requires that it be hit, rather than caught, held, or pushed.

When the first two players cross the initial line have Players 3 and 4 stand and begin striking the balloon without having it stop in between. Have other players stand in turn and repeat the same procedure. Award five points to each pair who completes the relay. Have pairs deduct one point from their scores for each time the balloon comes to a rest (by holding or pushing it) and for each time a player hits the balloon twice in succession. Do not penalize players for balloons that hit the floor, since the difficulty of striking them in that position is penalty enough.

(79) BALLOON TRAPPING

Description

Goals: Utilize coordination.
              Cooperate with partner.

Alignment: Sitting in lines all facing the same direction.

Movements: Running, walking.

Equipment: One 10- to 12-inch balloon per group with extra balloons
              available, two cones per group.

Social   Competitive.
  structure: 4-6 people per group, ages 7 to 12.

Directions

Instruct the first two people in each line to stand and trap the balloon between their bodies. On signal, have players walk down around the cone and back without (a) letting the balloon fall, and (b) touching it with the hands or wrists. If the balloon falls, have players use their hands to resituate it before continuing on. For any other time that players touch the balloon with the hands, have that pair start over. If a pair touches the balloon with the hands after making it half way, have them start over from the midpoint. Instruct other players to stand in turn, two at a time, and repeat the same procedure. Award teams one point for each pair that completes the relay.

(80) BALLOON PUSHING

Description

Goals: Utilize coordination and timing.

Alignment: Sitting in lines all facing the same direction.

Movements: Pushing, walking.

Equipment: One 10- to 12-inch balloon and paper plate per person, with extra balloons available, two cones per group.

Social
structure: Competitive and cooperative.
4-6 people per group, ages 7 to 12.

Directions

Instruct the first person in each line to stand and receive a balloon and paper plate. On signal, have players walk down around the cone and back while pushing the balloon with the plate. If players touch the balloon with the hands or other body parts, or strike the balloon with the plate, have them begin again. If players touch the balloon in error after making it half way, have them start over from the midpoint. Instruct other players to stand in turn, and begin when the prior teammate reaches the far cone. Award teams one point for each person who completes the relay.

Note: Use sturdy paper or Styrofoam plates that will keep their shape throughout the activity.

(81) TANDEM SCOOT

Description

Goals: Respect and trust others.
              Improve agility.

Alignment: Sitting, kneeling, or laying on a scooter behind a line
              while linked with partner.

Movements: Grasping, scooting.

Equipment: Two scooters per group.

Social   Cooperative within competitive.
   structure: 4-6 players per group, ages 7 to 12.

Directions

Challenge players two at a time to advance their scooters around the marker and back while remaining linked in some way (i.e. linking elbows while sitting; joining hands and ankles while laying down). If players unlink at any moment, have players begin again from behind the initial line. If players unlink after making it half way, have them begin again from the midpoint.

Note: Caution players to avoid standing on scooters and to keep hands free of the wheels at all times.

Alternative: Repeat the activity with all players in a different position on the scooter.

(82) TIRE JUMPING

Description

Goals: Practice broad jump.
Strengthen leg muscles.
Understand need to toss tire far enough to enable long jumps, yet close enough to complete jumps.

Alignment: Sitting in lines all facing the same direction.

Movements: Jumping, tossing.

Equipment: One bicycle tire per group.

Social
  structure: Competitive.
3-4 people per group, ages 7 to 12.

Directions

Place a bicycle tire for each group on the floor behind the starting line. Line up groups behind their respective tires, with the first person in each line standing inside the tire. On signal, have the first people slide the tires out from under their feet and toss them as far as possible, yet close enough so they may still jump into them. Instruct players to jump by taking off with one or two feet and landing on two feet. Have active players continue alternately tossing the tires and jumping into the center as fast as they are able. Have players who fail to jump into a tire from their previous spot begin again behind the starting line. Have someone who fails to jump into a tire after making it half way begin again from the midpoint.

(83) WHOSE SHOE

Description

Goals: Cooperate with others.
                     Communicate with others.

Alignment: Sitting in lines facing center, equal distance from the
                     center.

Movements: Running, tying or fastening shoes.

Equipment: Two shoes per person.

Social   Cooperative and competitive.
    structure: 3-4 people per group, ages 7 to 12.

Directions

Instruct all players to untie (or unfasten) and remove one shoe, passing it up to the first person in line (Player 1). Have Player 1 take the shoes and put them in a common pile in the center of the playing area. Mix the shoes up well, continuing to stir them periodically until activity begins (so players are unaware of the location of particular shoes).

On signal, instruct the first person in each line to stand and run to the center to retrieve the shoe of any teammate. Have the player that "belongs" to that shoe put it on entirely (including tying or fastening) and run to retrieve another teammate's shoe. Continue the process until all players are wearing their shoes and sitting down in line. Allow players to shout any directions to teammates they find helpful, as long as all players but the retriever remain behind the starting line.

Note: Spread out people with shoes that do not tie or fasten as evenly as possible across groups, since they can put them on more easily.

(84) PICNIC PANTRY

Description

Goals: Exercise total body intermittently.
Communicate with partner.

Alignment: Sitting in lines all facing the same direction.

Movements: Placing, running.

Equipment: One picnic basket (or box) and corresponding items per group, suggested items listed below.

Social structure: Cooperative within competitive.
4-6 people per group, ages 7 to 12.

Directions

Place a basket or box of picnic items across from each group behind the endline. Instruct the first two people in each group to run to their basket, get the tablecloth, spread it out behind the endline, and return to the back of the line. When these players return, have the next two people retrieve four of any item from the basket, set them up on the tablecloth and return. Have remaining players follow the same procedure until all items have been placed on the tablecloth. With small groups and two players moving at a time, each player will get at least two turns. Groups with an odd number of players will have a different partner for each turn.

Possible items in baskets (four of each, except table cloth):

Tablecloth	Forks
Paper plates	Spoons
Bowls	Fake or plastic food items
Cups	Napkins

Alternative: After the relay is completed once, the picnic set-up could be dismantled in reverse order during a second round.

(85) MOUNTAIN TRIATHLON

Description

Goals: Exercise entire body intermittently.

Alignment: Sitting in small groups behind sideline of basketball court.

Movements: Scooting, simulated climbing and skiing.

Equipment: One scooter and cone per group, two polydots per group to mark positions two and three.

Social   Competitive.
   structure: 4-6 players per group, ages 7-12.

Directions

Disperse equipment to teams and spread out each team so the first three players may be active as depicted in Figure 7.2 (p. 139). Instruct players to complete the following activities in unison while in their corresponding positions. Although Player 1 is the first participant in the actual relay, players might best think of the activities in reverse order:

Player 1: The first participant depicts swimming across a mountain lake by lying down on a scooter and propelling herself down around a cone and back (the width of a basketball court).

Player 2: While the first person swims the lake, the second player depicts skiing down the mountain. The movement is characterized by doing repetitive slalom jumps sideways back and forth over a polydot.

Player 3: While the first person swims the lake, the third player depicts climbing up the mountain. The movement is characterized by doing the mountain climber callisthenic (extending one leg backward from a squatting position; then repetitively alternating which leg is extended backward).

Note: The second and third players in line need enough room to complete their assigned activities.

(86) TIRE TOSS

Description

Goals: Practice underhand tossing.

Alignment: Standing in small groups behind sideline of
                  basketball court.

Movements: Retrieving, tossing.

Equipment: One bicycle tire per group, one beanbag per person,
                  masking tape.

Social   Competitive.
structure: 3-5 players per group, ages 8-12.

Directions

Place a small piece of tape on the floor about five feet in front of each group, and additional pieces of tape in front of each line in three-foot increments (5-6 pieces of tape for each group, indicated by squares in Diagram 7.1). Place a tire so it surrounds the first piece of tape for each group. Have the first player from each line try to toss a beanbag into the tire, followed by each teammate in succession tossing a beanbag. If no more than one person in a group misses his toss, the group advances the tire to the next mark and repeats the sequence. If more than one person misses a toss for any given round, all players in that group repeat their tosses to the tire in that same location (as many times as necessary). The object for each group is to advance its tire as far as possible across the court. The activity is not a race as in many other relays.

Diagram 7.1

Tire Toss

(87) GIVE 'N TAKE

Description

Goals: Exercise total body intermittently.
                Improve agility.

Alignment: Sitting in rows near the corners of a square, facing the
                center.

Movements: Collecting, placing, running.

Equipment: One bicycle tire per group, one center tire with
                three times more beanbags than the number of groups.

Social   Competitive.
structure: 4-6 players per group, 3-5 groups, ages 8 to 12.

Directions

Instruct Player 1 from each group to run and take a beanbag from the
center tire, then run back and place it in her tire. Tell the runner to sit
down at the end of her line (see Team Z in Diagram 7.2). When the
beanbag is resting in the tire, have Player 2 from each group take a
beanbag from the center tire and bring it back. When the center tire is
depleted, have runners take beanbags from other team's tires, indicated by
Team X in the diagram. Tell those sitting to gradually slide to the right
so they may run up the diagonal lines on their turns. Repeat turns as
necessary until the moment one group has six beanbags placed down in
its tire. Since one round takes only a few minutes, play two to three
rounds.

Alternative: Vary the number of beanbags required to finish to make the
game longer or shorter.

Diagram 7.2
Give 'n Take

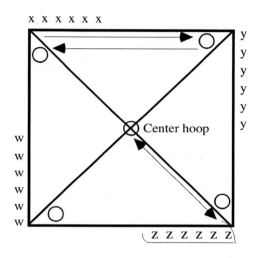

Diagram 7.3
Crisscross

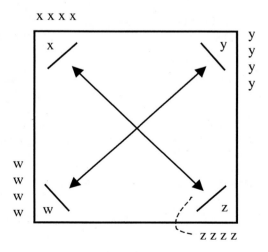

(88) CRISSCROSS

Description

Goals: Exercise total body intermittently.
                Utilize hand-eye coordination.
                Practice dribbling.
                Understand need to dribble quickly, yet under control.

Alignment: Standing in files outside the corners of a square; first
                person behind a restraining line, facing the center.

Movements: Dodging, dribbling.

Equipment: One basketball per group.

Social   Competitive.
  structure: 3-7 players per group, ages 8 to 12.

Directions

Arrange groups as shown in Diagram 7.3 and give each an appropriate sized basketball. Instruct the first person in each group to dribble the ball diagonally across the square, hand it to the next player in the opposite group, and stand at the end of the opposite line (four players crisscross simultaneously; Player X joins the Team Z line as noted with curved line in diagram). Instruct ensuing players to complete the same pattern as quickly as possible, but under control. As each player begins dribbling, have the next player in line move into position behind the restraining line. The team that returns all players to their initial positions first is the winner.

Note: With six or seven players per team, have the third and fourth people in line perform a callisthenic while waiting as described on p. 138.

Alternative: To vary the skill, substitute a soccer ball or floor hockey stick and puck for the basketball. Require players to stop movement of the equipment without using hands before the next player proceeds (players are less likely to dribble equipment out of control if they are solely responsible for stopping it at the other end).

(89) BUCKET BRIGADE

Description

Goals: Cooperate with others.
Understand strategy of passing cups quickly, yet without spilling water.

Alignment: Standing in lines equally spaced between two buckets.

Movements: Handing, grasping, pouring cups of water.

Equipment: Two buckets and two (6-8 people) or three (9-11 people) cups per group with extra cups available, hose for filling buckets.

Social
   structure: Cooperative within competitive.
6-9 people per group, ages 8 to 14.

Directions

On signal, instruct Player 1 to dip a cup into a bucket filled with water and pass it down the line. When the cup reaches the end of the line, have that person pour it into the empty bucket and send it the reverse direction down the line. At the same time the first cup is poured into the bucket, have Player 1 fill and pass a second cup. While passing cups both directions, require every person in line to handle each cup (no person may be skipped).

Have each group continue filling their buckets until the water overflows or reaches a designated mark, depending on bucket size. Give any group a replacement cup upon request by exchanging it at the beginning of the line.

(90) TIRE CHAIN

Description

Goals:	Communicate with others. Solve problem. Practice balancing.
Alignment:	Standing in small groups behind sideline of basketball court.
Movements:	Balancing, passing.
Equipment:	One more automobile tire than the number of people in group.
Social structure:	Cooperative. 6-9 people, ages 9 to 14.

Directions

Stack tires in any manner behind the sideline. Instruct the group to use the tires to advance all its members across the court beyond the other sideline (or about 50 feet) without (a) touching the floor until advancing beyond the far sideline, and (b) having more than one player on a tire at a time. If any parameter is violated, the group must begin again.

(91) SHOE SCRAMBLE

Description

Goals: Cooperate with others.

Alignment: Sitting in a circle facing the center.

Movements: Passing, tying shoes.

Equipment: One shoe of each person.

Social Cooperative or competitive.
structure: 8-16 people per circle, ages 9 to 14.

Directions

Instruct players to untie or unfasten one shoe, then remove it and place it in a box. Position someone else's shoe behind each player. On signal, have all players take the shoe from behind and hand it to the left. Permit players to pass only one shoe at a time, and only one position at a time (i.e. without skipping people). When a player receives his own shoe, have him put it on intermittently while continuing to pass shoes. The game is completed when all players are wearing both shoes that are tied or fastened. Score the game by how fast groups finish relative to others (competitive) or relative to a previous time (cooperative).

Alternative: For additional challenge, periodically change the direction players pass shoes while in progress.

(92) IN SYNC

Description

Goals: Practice free throws and lay-ups in game situation.
                Experience large muscle movement intermittently.

Alignment: Standing in line front-to-back at free throw line.

Movements: Shooting free throws and lay-ups, rebounding, jogging.

Equipment: Two basketballs and one polydot per group.

Social   Competitive and cooperative.
   structure: 4-5 players per group, 4-6 groups, ages 9 to 14.

Directions

Divide players into groups of four or five. Line up each group at the free throw line of its own basket and give each two basketballs. Instruct the first player in each group to attempt a free throw. Have those who make the shot immediately rebound the ball and pass it to the third shooter, before jogging to the end of the line. Have first shooters who miss the free throw attempt any short shot (usually a lay-up) until one is made.

As soon as the initial free throw is attempted, have the second shooter attempt a free throw and repeat the same sequence. Each shooter tries to remain "in sync" by making a shot (long or short) prior to the subsequent shooter. When a shooter behind a player makes a shot before the shooter in front, the shooter in front, or "out of sync," rotates to the next basket clockwise. Score the game by the number of rotations each player makes (fewer is better).

Note: Require players to bounce-pass the ball to shooters in line and jog a wide path around the line to avoid interfering with other shooters.

Alternative: Depending on ability of players, place a polydot three feet in front of the free throw line and allow players to choose their "free throw" distance.

(93) T-SHIRTS ON PARADE

Description

Goals: Practice striking.
                Utilize eye-hand coordination.

Alignment: Sitting in lines all facing the same direction.

Movements: One- or two-hand striking, putting on and removing t-shirt.

Equipment: One t-shirt and one 10- to 12-inch balloon per group
                with extra balloons available, two cones per group.

Social   Competitive.
structure: 3-4 people per group, ages 10 to 14.

Directions

Seat groups down behind their respective cones, and place a second cone about five feet in front of each group. Give the first person (Player 1) in each line a blown up balloon and t-shirt. On signal, instruct Player 1 to take the balloon and t-shirt out to the second cone. Have Player 1 strike the balloon repetitively without letting it hit the floor, while trying to put on the t-shirt at the same time. The head and arms must go through the appropriate openings and the shirt needs to be pulled down to the waist (but it may be backwards or inside out). Once the shirt is on, Player 1 removes the shirt while keeping the balloon in the air. When the shirt is removed Player 1 takes the balloon and shirt to Player 2 and sits down at the back of the line (and so on).

Penalize players one point for every time the balloon hits the floor (points are undesirable). Each time the balloon hits the floor a player may choose to put in or take out one body part, respectively while the balloon is on the floor.

Note: All t-shirts must be large enough for all players to spare someone embarrassment from not fitting into a shirt.

(94) LAP TAG

Description

Goals: Exercise total body intermittently.

Alignment: Standing in lines at corners of area.

Movements: Running, tagging.

Equipment: Two cones per group, one baton or deck ring per group.

Social   Competitive.
  structure: 4-6 people per group, ages 10 to 14.

Directions

Instruct the first person in each group to run a lap and tag his next teammate, and so on. The next runner may leave immediately or wait until a passing runner from another team advances beyond his 2nd cone (in Diagram 7.4, Runner X waited for Runner W to pass the 2nd cone [open triangle]). Any runner who is tagged from the rear by another team joins that group at the back of the line, and the next runner from the tagged player's team initiates its running sequence again from the home cone (solid triangles). Teams earn one point for each runner in their respective groups (relative to the number they began with) when activity is stopped.

Diagram 7.4

Lap Tag

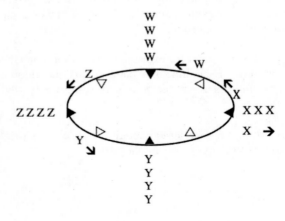

Chapter 8

Game Administration

This book is devoted to the subject of game content and ways to administrate game content in order to include all children and adolescents. In a sense, game administration involves monitoring game elements, one of the topics discussed in chapter 2. Although there are more peripheral responsibilities associated with game administration than monitoring game elements, they are nonetheless important. This chapter addresses some "how to's" of selected peripheral responsibilities that occur before, during, or following a game. The companion book (Henkel, 2010) also closes with a chapter on game administration or management, but with a focus on key conditions for prioritizing game outcomes.

Pregame Responsibilities

Pregame responsibilities include setting up a game, determining groups, getting equipment, and explaining the game. Each of these responsibilities may be carried out effectively if leaders have first planned well. Planning involves familiarizing oneself with games in advance, and selecting games that are developmentally appropriate for a particular group of players. Leaders also need to familiarize themselves with the recreational facility and space available. Aspects of the physical space often suggest safety considerations and how to best set up a game.

Setting up Game

Games requiring set-up may be prepared by a teacher or other leader, or by capable players under the direction of a leader. Set-up most often involves laying out boundaries and organizing equipment for tasks involving locomotion, nonlocomotion, object control or sport skills. Setting up a game before a group arrives maximizes playing time and achieves better organization and control. When a large group needs to wait for a game to be set up, some players fill their time by bothering others. Sometimes leaders may want to share responsibility for setting up with players, particularly when games cannot be set up in advance. The longer the game time allotted, the more leaders can sacrifice a few minutes to let players help.

Determining Groups

Groups should be determined in a way that does not single out players. Instead of choosing players with captains, leaders may use arbitrary criteria. The most common arbitrary criteria is having players "count off," using one number for each group needed. So, if four groups are needed, players count from 1 through 4 until all receive a number. Leaders need to be sure players do not intentionally change their positions in line to receive a particular number. When assigning younger children numbers leaders may wish to disperse them to team locations as counting occurs. Otherwise, players may forget groupings before counting is complete.

Other criteria for determining groups include birthdays (by month), eye color, or number of letters in the last name. When selected criteria do not evenly determine groups, a leader may ask a couple of people to change groups. When this occurs, players are not singled out by ability, since they know anyone could be asked to change.

In games for two people, leaders may encourage players to find a partner of equal ability. The following guideline helps include all players: "If someone asks you to be a partner, the answer is always yes." Then if a few people have not found partners after a short while, the leader may quietly assign them so no attention shifts to players without a partner. Leaders may also use a matched-pair exercise occasionally, in which a slip of paper is handed to each player with the name of a person or thing. Then players are instructed to find the person with the matching slip. Examples include historical figures (i.e. Lewis & Clark), fictitious characters (i.e. Mickey & Minnie), and foods or other items (i.e. peanut butter & jelly).

Rotating groups can be equally important as determining them initially. The impact of a child's participation on a particular team is lessened when team make-up changes regularly. Some games require regular rotation, such as *Advantage* (p. 86) and *Link Ball* (p. 126). Other times leaders may rotate players during the same activity or in between activities. In games for two people, children could play one round with an initial partner, and successive rounds with different partners. In an activity involving more than two teams, a given team may face different opponents. In addition to rotating opponents, leaders are encouraged to change the make-up of teams so a given team does not always win or lose.

Explaining Game

When explaining games, initial comments should cover the most critical aspects only. Then players may begin moving without a long delay. Critical aspects of a game include the main goal(s), primary rules, and safety considerations.

Leaders cannot assume children understand the goal(s) of a game. Leaders often alert players to motor skills or scoring strategies involved in a game, yet assume players will cooperate without specific directions. Cooperative skills, such as helping others and communicating respectfully, need to be directly taught in the same manner as other game skills. Deline (1991) and Hellison (1987) remind us that children are often uncooperative because they lack specific skills, not because they lack desire to cooperate. One way to teach cooperative skills is by assigning roles to various group members. Glover and Midura (1995, 1992) suggest the roles of organizer, praiser, encourager, summarizer and recorder. Naturally, the roles may be changed to fit a particular activity. A leader may assign a conflict manager for one activity and forego the role of recorder. Regardless which roles are encouraged, individual accountability is important in achieving the goals of a game. Grineski (1996) describes various ways to hold students accountable, including randomly asking them to explain some aspect of an activity to a leader, and having students teach part of a game to peers.

In addition to the goal(s) of a game, kids need to know primary rules and safety considerations before playing. The more complex a game, the more the initial explanation should include "chalk talk" or "walk through" examples. Children more fully understand positioning of players and options with equipment when they see, as well as hear, examples. A chalk talk is a way to visually diagram game information in a short time. A walk through example requires more time, but is more concrete than a chalk talk, because selected players physically model aspects of the game.

After leaders have explained primary rules and safety considerations of a game, children can play briefly to determine what they understand. Then secondary rules can be added and further questions may be asked. A primary rule for *Scatter Dodgeball* (p. 114) is to hit other players below the shoulders to insure safety. By contrast, not allowing players to have more than one ball at a time is a secondary rule, since the information is not necessary for people to initially try the game.

Getting Equipment

In some cases, game equipment can be laid in position before players arrive, thereby maximizing time to play. Since this scenario is likely the exception, game leaders need a variety of other ways to disperse equipment, while considering the amount and kind used. Generally speaking, it is most advantageous to allocate equipment as the last step before actually beginning play. Then equipment is not a distraction while explaining other procedures. When players do get their own equipment they can be dismissed in groups to avoid congestion. Minimizing distraction can also be accomplished after groups get equipment by including a concrete direction as part of the procedures: "Girls, you are about to get a ball. As soon as you're standing in your own space with the ball still, I'll know we can start the game...Go...Boys..."

Game Responsibilities

Game responsibilities occur after an activity is under way. Key responsibilities include monitoring time, refereeing and encouraging children.

Monitoring Time

Monitoring time is a responsibility closely linked to including all players in a game. If time expires before all players get to perform some skill, those who did not get a turn feel cheated. In *Kickball*, for instance, everyone needs a chance to kick the ball because kicking is the central skill in the game. In some games, however, time does not permit each child to perform the central skill, or several skills are incorporated to equal degrees. In these cases, all children do not necessarily need to perform all skills or play all positions. An example of time constraints occurs in *Rhythmical Red Light* (p. 102). If each child takes a turn beating the drum, a group of 20 children will require about 60 minutes to play, which is far too prohibitive. An example of multiple skills or positions occurs in *Link Ball* (p. 126). All players need not play as shaggers in the end zone, since they are equally active playing other positions.

Modifying rules helps a leader conserve time. To insure that all children kick the ball in *Kickball*, leaders may have each player on a team kick before switching that team to the field. Eliminating the three outs saves transition time required to switch teams, since teams switch less frequently. An additional benefit is that a player's out does not cause her team to switch to the field. Kicking and fielding opportunities may be increased further by utilizing two kickers at a time as in *Double Trouble* (p. 133). In that activity, two kickers are involved at a time by running opposite directions around the bases. Consequently, fielders gain twice as many opportunities to play the ball.

Another important aspect of monitoring time involves stoppage of play. A leader may wonder how long children need to play a game to achieve the goals. Two general principles are to (a) provide variety by playing more than one game, and (b) stop a game when interest is high. Whether or not these principles may be accomplished depends on the game. *Link Ball* (p. 126) is designed as an ongoing game with considerable strategy. The strategy normally takes players at least 15 minutes to understand and implement. By contrast, one round of *Everybody It* (p. 110) requires only about 45 seconds. Therefore, *Link Ball* would probably require the entire class time allotted, whereas *Everybody It* could be played several times, and still move on to one or two other games. Another factor determining game length is familiarity. On the average, unfamiliar games take longer than familiar games because more time for explanation is required. Therefore, leaders are better off to play one familiar and one unfamiliar game on the same day, rather than attempting two unfamiliar games.

Refereeing

Refereeing is best done by children and adolescents as they play so the game leader is free to observe and comment as needed. A second reason for helping children referee their own games is that adults are not always present when children play. Since play occurs during recess and at home when adults do not immediately oversee the activity, children need practice interpreting rules and settling problems.

A third reason for having players referee their own games is to develop character. Even if adults were always available to settle problems among children, this is not in the best interests of helping children mature. For children to act as responsible adults they need to assume increasing responsibility for interacting with peers and making decisions.   Adults can guide them in this process by helping them distinguish between a respectful and a disrespectful response to a leader, or between an encouraging and discouraging response to a teammate.

Naturally, refereeing one's own games is a developmental process. Children cannot just be thrown into an activity and be told to referee fairly. They need modeling by adults and specific guidelines for making decisions. Without singling out individuals publicly, leaders can appeal to players to sacrifice their pride or other personal desire to rule in favor of an opponent. Solving problems in this manner takes time. Leaders need to balance this problem solving approach with expedient problem solving. If players take time to work through each little dispute the flow of the game is interrupted too often.

Sometimes expedient solutions can be built right into game rules so the leader does not necessarily need to intervene. In tagging games, for example, players can be taught the guideline that the tagger can simply decide whether another player was actually tagged.   The concrete guideline gives players opportunities to be trustworthy and reduces the tendency for arguing. Additional guidelines for character development that may be applied to refereeing are discussed in chapter 4 of the companion book (Henkel, 2010).

Encouraging Players

Leaders need to carefully observe a game to determine what kind of experience players are having. Careful observation involves seeing all aspects of a game, and not just intense activity surrounding the ball or other equipment. Chapter 2 suggests ways to modify games based on what occurs. Whether or not a leader actually modifies a game, the leader has an important role as an encourager. Giving encouragement affirms players for accomplishing some aspect of a game.

Examples of affirmative responses are given in Table 8.1. Items 1 through 32 are general superlatives that potentially motivate players. Leaders are encouraged to give more specific information when time permits. A leader may affirm skill performance (Items 34-38), strategy (Items 39-41), attitude (Items 42-44), or effort (Items 45-49). Using a variety of responses helps players receive comments more sincerely. In addition to affirming children, leaders may correct a player's performance, or suggest what can be done differently. Corrections tend to carry a negative connotation, since they emphasize what someone did not do in the past, rather than what the person can do in the future:

Correction: "You didn't get under the ball far enough."
Suggestion: "Try to get under the ball a little further."

Table 8.1

Ways to Affirm Players

Superlatives

1. Awesome!
2. Beautiful!
3. Clever!
4. Congratulations!
5. Cool!
6. Dynamite!
7. Exactly!
8. Excellent!
9. Exceptional!
10. Fabulous!
11. Fantastic!
12. Fine!
13. Gorgeous!
14. Great!
15. Incredible!
16. Magnificent!
17. Marvelous!
18. Nice!
19. Outstanding!
20. Sensational!
21. Sharp!
22. Spectacular!
23. Splendid!
24. Super!
25. Superb!
26. Sweet!
27. Swell!
28. Terrific!
29. Tremendous!
30. Wonderful!
31. Wow!
32. Yes!

Specific affirmation: Skill

34. Good job following through.
35. Good move.
36. Way to get under the ball.
37. That was right on the money.
38. Your timing was great.

Specific affirmation: Strategy

39. Good job talking to each other.
40. Now you've figured out a plan.
41. Way to look for a teammate.

Specific affirmation: Attitude

42. Good patience.
43. Good self-control.
44. Thanks for not arguing.

Specific affirmation: Effort

45. Keep it up.
46. One more time and you'll have it.
47. You did a lot of work today.
48. You're really trying hard.
49. You've just about got it.

How not to affirm players

50. Practice makes perfect.
51. That's a good girl.
52. That's not bad.
53. You finally got it.

Corrections and suggestions tend to be received better when they follow affirmations:

> Affirmation: "Nice hustle getting to the ball."
> Suggestion: "Next time see if you can also get under it more."

Even when leaders give players many affirmative responses, they need to guard against sending hidden messages. Items 50 through 53 in Table 8.1 provide examples of hidden messages. Hidden messages may (a) encourage pursuing an unrealistic goal, (b) focus on a child's personhood, (c) be misdirected, or (d) be sarcastic. An unrealistic goal is represented by Item 50. If a child really believes enough practice leads to perfection (as opposed to improvement), the child may also believe anything less than perfection is unacceptable. Item 51 refers to a child's personhood, rather than performance. Even though the response is positive, it incorrectly suggests that a person's value changes with performance. A misdirected response is represented by Item 52. The focus is on what the performance is not (bad), instead of on what the performance is (good). A person who interprets the statement literally will realize that a lot of mediocrity can be sandwiched between good and bad. Item 53 carries an element of sarcasm. Telling a child, "You finally got it" contains the possible hidden message, "It's about time"!

A leader's role in encouraging players extends to the players themselves. Modeling a variety of ways to give encouragement and directly prodding children can help them to encourage one another. The less experience players have in this role, the more leaders need to reinforce and reward the goal of encouraging peers in a game. Rewards and other postgame responsibilities are discussed in the next section.

Postgame responsibilities

Playing a game can be fun and exciting. In addition to the activity itself, part of the value of a game occurs after it is over. Postgame responsibilities help bring closure to the game experience. Players need closure to reinforce learning and as a transition before they move on to their next endeavor. Specific responsibilities following a game may include returning equipment, discussing the activity, and, for certain special events, giving rewards.

Returning Equipment

Returning equipment usually occurs during the transition between game stoppage and discussion, when player's excitement and emotions are still recovering. They may be thinking about a confusing rule or controversial play. An extra adult may assume responsibility for returning equipment, so the game leader can be free to monitor groups as they sit down together or separately. If an extra adult is not available, responsible players may return equipment, as long as directions are clear, and they finish in time to join the closing discussion. As with dispersing equipment, players may return it in groups to avoid congestion and possible wear and tear on equipment: "Squads 1 and 2 may return their balloons and come sit by me" (and so on).

Discussing Activity

Discussing a game following activity helps achieve three purposes. First of all, discussion can help players more fully understand a game. If a player misunderstands a particular rule or strategy, the problem is best cleared up right away, rather than the next time the game is played.

Secondly, discussion helps reinforce the goals of a game. Leaving children with a key principle concerning skills or values provides the best chance that they will apply the same principle in another setting. If a problem occurs during a game, such as players cheating, discussion should not wait until the end of the game. Instead, the leader can stress the importance of honesty for the remainder of the game, without singling out a particular individual.

A third purpose of discussing a game is to boost the self-esteem of players. Children who think they did poorly need to hear the leader remind the group that each person is different and trying one's best is the most that can be expected.

Discussion should not be long and drawn out. In fact, a long discussion runs counter to the main purpose of playing a game—to be active. The leader may choose to focus on one of the purposes above, and emphasize a different purpose on another occasion. Over time, all three purposes may be achieved collectively.

Rewarding Players

Rewarding people for their accomplishments in games communicates that their activities are important and that leaders care about their performance. Certainly people are rewarded in other settings for other accomplishments, though often in intangible ways. While rewarding players tangibly at times is appropriate, leaders also need to structure rewards to avoid the following possible shortcomings.

Distributing rewards unevenly

If a lot of emphasis is placed on rewards, and one team seldom earns rewards, they may quit trying. Changing the make-up of teams can help insure that all people earn some rewards, but other shortcomings still warrant consideration.

Giving rewards too frequently

Players who receive rewards often may become too extrinsically motivated. They may lose interest in working toward a goal unless a reward is given. Intrinsic motivation can be enhanced by giving rewards some of the time, and other times simply emphasizing that learning is fun and helps a person grow. Over time, rewards can be given less often and still be motivating.

Esteeming rewards too highly

Children have a difficult time separating performance from personhood. Their self-esteems can be influenced markedly by performance. Varying the criteria for giving rewards helps all children succeed. Criteria can help reinforce the importance of what occurs during a game, as well as the outcome of a game. It is inconsistent to tell children the goals of a game are to play hard and have fun, yet reward the "winners." Alternative criteria for rewards include:

   a. Abiding by game rules.
   b. Playing a game safely.
   c. Saying encouraging comments to teammates.
   d. Demonstrating unusual effort.

If leaders still wish to occasionally reward the outcome of a game, rewards need not compare one team to another. Additional criteria include:

   d. Having larger team attendance than the previous day.
   e. Scoring more team points than the previous day.
   f. Scoring more combined team points than the previous day.

Using inclusive criteria like those suggested has implications for leaders who plan and distribute rewards. Since more people would potentially meet the criteria, more money would be spent on rewards, and more rewards would need to be available on a given day or night.

Closing

Success for Kids in Active Games is written to encourage leaders to carefully determine the games children and adolescents play. The elements of a game are described to provide alternatives for making games age appropriate, yet flexible, so players of different ability levels may enjoy a high level of success. The book also gives recommendations for developing a healthy self-esteem among players by distinguishing between their personhood and their performance, and by monitoring the conditions under which players are expected to compete. Most of the conditions have to do with monitoring the structure of an activity and the attitudes of players.

Many games and relays are included for different sized groups so leaders may select activities that have worked in other settings before. While I anticipate leaders utilizing many of the games provided, my hope and prayer is that leaders—and players themselves—will design new games using the same principles.

Since the scope of this book is necessarily focused, some complementary ideas are contained in another book, *Integrating Active Games with Other Subjects* (Henkel, 2010). Based on the same foundational principles, that book presents 67 games that integrate physical activity with the subjects of language arts, math, science, social studies, culture, and character development. Although the topics of culture and character development are not commonly viewed as core subjects, they are integrated with movement due to the ongoing attention the topics receive in schools and other public arenas, and due to the potential of games to incorporate related principles effectively. Whether applying the ideas of this book or the complementary book, I wish you God's speed as you do so with the best interests of players in mind.

BIBLIOGRAPHY

Ames, C. (1984). Achievement attributions and self-instructions under competitive and individualistic goal structures. *Journal of Educational Psychology, 76* (3), 478-487.

Baumgarten, S. (1988). Nothing short of a revolution. *Journal of Physical Education, Recreation and Dance, 59* (2), 38-41.

Bavolek, S. (1993). *Child centered coaching parent handbook: Having fun and feeling good about me.* Park City, UT: Family Nurturing Center.

Belka, D. (1999). Games to consider avoiding. *Teaching Elementary Physical Education, 10* (3), 16, 30.

Bredemeier, B., & Shields, D. (1984). Divergence in moral reasoning about sport and everyday life. *Sociology of Sport Journal, 1*, 348-357.

Bredemeier, B., & Shields, D. (1986). Game reasoning and interactional morality. *Journal of Genetic Psychology, 147*, 257-275.

Brown, L., & Grineski, S. (1992). Competition in physical education: An educational contradiction? *Journal of Physical Education, Recreation and Dance, 63* (1), 17-19.

Coakley, J. (1990). *Sport in society: Issues and controversies.* St. Louis: Times Mirror/Mosby.

Deline, J. (1991). Why...can't they get along? *Journal of Physical Education, Recreation and Dance, 62* (1), 21-26.

Dobson, J. (2001). *The new hide or seek: Building confidence in your child.* Grand Rapids, MI: Revell.

Duda, R. (1981). *A cross-cultural analysis of achievement motivation in sport and the classroom.* Unpublished doctoral dissertation, University of Illinois, Champaign-Urbana.

Dweck, C., & Elliott, E. (1984). Achievement motivation. In M. Hetherington (Ed.), *Social development: Carmichael's manual of child psychology,* 643-691. New York: Wiley.

Fraleigh, W. (1984). *Right actions in sport.* Champaign, IL: Human Kinetics.

Glover, D., & Midura, D. (1992). *Team building through physical challenges.* Champaign, IL: Human Kinetics.

Gould, D. (1984). Psychosocial development and children's sport. In J.R. Thomas (Ed.), *Motor development during childhood and adolescence* (pp. 212-236). Minneapolis: Burgess.

Grineski, S. (1996). *Cooperative learning in physical education.* Champaign, IL: Human Kinetics.

Hellison, D. (1987). The affective domain in physical education—Let's do some housecleaning. *Journal of Physical Education, Recreation and Dance, 58* (6), 41-43.

Henkel, S. (2010). *Integrating active games with other subjects.* Cottage Grove, MN: MGB Printing.

Henkel, S. (2007). Honoring God through sports competition. *Journal of Christian Education, 50* (2), 33-43.

Henkel, S. (1997). Monitoring competition for success. *Journal of Physical Education, Recreation and Dance, 68* (2), 21-28.

Henkel, S. (1995). *Games for success: Developing childrens' character through recreational play.* Lanham, MD: University Press of America.

Huizinga, J. (1955). *Homo ludens: A study of the play element in culture.* Boston: Beacon.

Johnson, D., & Maruyama, G. et al. (1981). Effects of cooperative, competitive, and individualistic goal structures on achievement: A meta-analysis. *Psychological Bulletin, 89* (1), 47-62.

Kohn, A. (1992). *No contest: The case against competition.* New York: Houghton Mifflin.

Lentz, T., & Cornelius, R. (1950). *All together: A manual of cooperative games*. St. Louis, MO: Peace Research Laboratory.

Martens, R. (1978). *Joy and sadness in children's sports*. Champaign, IL: Human Kinetics.

Mauldon, E., & Redfern, H. (1981). *Games teaching: An approach to the primary school*. London: MacDonald & Evans.

McDowell, J. (1993). *His image, my image*. Nashville, TN: Thomas Nelson.

Midura, D., & Glover, D. (1999). *The competition-cooperation link*. Champaign, IL: Human Kinetics.

Midura, D., & Glover, D. (1995). *More team building challenges*. Champaign, IL: Human Kinetics.

Morris, G., & Stiehl, J. (1999). *Changing kids games*. Champaign, IL: Human Kinetics.

National Association for Sport and Physical Activity (NASPE, 2004). *Moving into the future: National standards for physical education*. McGraw-Hill.

O'Brian, M. (1987). *Vince: A personal biography of Vince Lombardi*. New York: Morrow and Company.

Orlick, T. (1978). *Winning through cooperation: Competitive insanity, cooperative alternatives*. Washington, D.C.: Acropolis.

Orlick, T. (1981). Positive socialization via cooperative games. *Developmental Psychology, 17* (4), 426-429.

Orlick, T. (1982). *The second cooperative sports and games book*. New York: Pantheon.

Pangrazi, R, (2001). *Dynamic physical education for elementary school children*, 13th ed. Boston: Allyn & Bacon.

Pangrazi, R. (1982). Physical education, self-concept, and achievement. *Journal of Physical Education, Recreation and Dance, 53* (9), 16-18.

Rainey, D., & Rainey, B. (1995). *The new building your mate's self-esteem*. Nashville, TN: Thomas Nelson.

Robinson, D. (1989). An attribution analysis of student demoralization in the physical education setting. *Journal of Educational Psychology, 55,* 27-36.

Schwager, S. (1992). Relay races: Are they appropriate for elementary physical education? *Journal of Physical Education, Recreation and Dance, 63* (6), 54-56.

Thorpe, R., & Bunker, D. (1986). *Rethinking games teaching*. Loughborough: University of Technology.

Tutko, T., & Bruns, W. (1976). *Winning is everything and other American myths*. New York: Macmillan.

Walker, S. (1980). *Winning: The psychology of competition*. New York: Norton.

Walsh, S. (1987, February 6). Comment: Karate class teaches parent the importance of sports. *The Gateway,* p.2.

Werner, P. (1989). Teaching games: A tactical perspective. *Journal of Physical Education, Recreation and Dance, 60* (3), 97-101.

Wessinger, N. (1994). "I hit a home run!" The lived meaning of scoring in games in physical education. *Quest, 46* (4), 425-439.

Williams, N. (1994). The physical education hall of shame, part II. *Journal of Physical Education, Recreation and Dance, 65* (2), 17-20.

Williams, N. (1992). The physical education hall of shame. *Journal of Physical Education, Recreation and Dance, 63* (6), 57-60.

Wilson, N. (1976). *The frequency and patterns of utilization of selected motor skills by third and fourth grade girls and boys in the game of kickball*. Unpublished master's project, University of Georgia.

INDEX OF GAMES *

NAME	NO.	PAGE	AGES	STANDARD
Games for Partners				
Busy bodies	1	38	5-9	1, 2
Fist list	2	39	5-10	1, 2, 5
Balloon keep away	3	40	5-11	1, 2
Half court	4	41	7-12	1
Fab grab	5	42	7-12	1, 2
Timely bounce	6	43	7-12	1, 2
Reaction ball	7	44	7-12	1
Butterfly four square	8	45	7-12	1, 5
Tandem toss	9	46	7-12	1, 2, 5
Down ball	10	48	8-12	1, 2
Out of sight	11	49	8-12	5
Keeping pace	12	51	8-14	1, 4, 5
Short court	13	52	9-14	1, 2
Back and force	14	53	9-14	1, 2
Balloon descent	15	54	9-14	1, 2
Small Group Games				
Clockwise four square	16	57	5-8	1, 5
Loop da hoop	17	58	5-up	1, 5
Monkey on a rope	18	60	7-10	1, 5
Four square rotation	19	62	7-11	1, 5
Centipede	20	63	7-11	1, 5
Alive and kickin'	21	64	7-11	1, 5
Human machinery	22	65	7-12	1, 2, 5
Barrel ball	23	67	7-12	1, 5
Lost in space	24	68	7-12	1, 4, 5
Fruit of the room	25	69	7-12	1, 2
Snap to it	26	70	7-12	1, 2
Invent a course	27	72	7-12	1, 5
Invent a game	28	74	7-14	1, 2, 5
Beach ball bop	29	75	7-14	1, 5

* Standards refer to six outcomes of physical education developed by the
  National Association for Sport and Physical Education (see p. 180).
  Standards 3 and 6 are not represented in the index since most any game
  may address these, depending on the emphasis and dialogue provided.

178

INDEX OF GAMES (cont.)

NAME	NO.	PAGE	AGES	STANDARD
Small Group Games				
Rope rescue	30	76	7-14	4, 5
Jam jumping	31	77	8-12	1, 4, 5
Fleece and flee	32	78	8-12	1, 5
Bingo bowling	33	79	8-12	1, 5
Exchange ball	34	81	8-12	1, 2, 5
The fly	35	82	8-12	1, 4
Corner ball	36	83	8-13	1
Blanket launch	37	84	8-14	5
Advantage	38	86	8-14	1, 4
Pass 'n move	39	87	8-14	1, 4
Disc golf	40	88	8-up	1, 5
Side-by-side	41	89	8-up	1, 2, 5
Sequence	42	90	9-up	1, 4, 5
Soccer sequence	43	91	9-up	1, 4, 5
Jugglemania	44	93	9-up	1, 5
Toxic treats	45	94	9-up	1, 4, 5
Once-catch volleyball	46	95	10-14	1
Frisbee frenzy	47	96	10-14	1, 5
Large Group Games				
Musical hoops	48	98	5-8	1, 5
Heads up	49	100	5-8	1, 5
Square soccer	50	101	5-8	1
Rhythmical red light	51	102	5-9	1, 2, 5
Raindrops	52	103	5-9	1, 5
Topsy turvy	53	104	5-up	4, 5
Around the horn	54	105	7-10	1, 2, 5
Dot ball	55	106	7-11	1, 2, 4, 5
Blockade	56	108	7-11	1
Scooter ball	57	109	7-12	1, 2
Everybody it	58	110	7-up	1, 5
Color tag	59	111	7-up	1, 5
Flag tag	60	112	7-up	1, 4, 5
Flag chasers	61	113	7-up	1, 4, 5
Scatter dodgeball	62	114	7-up	1, 2

INDEX OF GAMES (cont.)

NAME	NO.	PAGE	AGES	STANDARD
Large Group Games				
Mat ball	63	115	8-12	1, 2
Pin soccer	64	117	8-12	1, 2
Garbage ball	65	118	8-12	1, 2
Sideline basketball	66	120	8-12	1, 2, 5
Beach ball blast	67	121	8-12	1
Huddle up	68	122	8-14	1, 5
Chain tag	69	123	8-up	1, 4, 5
Dribble tag	70	125	8-up	1, 2
Link ball	71	126	9-14	1, 5
Quadrant ball	72	129	9-14	1
Caboose ball	73	130	9-14	1, 2, 5
Orbit	74	131	10-14	1, 5
Double trouble	75	133	10-14	1, 2, 5
Big base	76	134	10-14	1, 2, 4, 5
Frisbee frame	77	135	10-up	1, 2
Relay Games				
Balloon batting	78	143	7-12	1, 2, 5
Balloon trapping	79	144	7-12	1, 5
Balloon pushing	80	145	7-12	1
Tandem scoot	81	146	7-12	1, 5
Tire jumping	82	147	7-12	1, 2, 4
Whose shoe	83	148	7-12	5
Picnic pantry	84	149	7-12	5
Mountain triathlon	85	150	7-12	1, 4
Tire toss	86	151	8-12	1
Give 'n take	87	152	8-12	1, 4
Crisscross	88	154	8-12	1, 2
Bucket brigade	89	155	8-14	2, 5
Tire chain	90	156	9-14	1, 5
Shoe scramble	91	157	9-14	5
In sync	92	158	9-14	1
T-shirts on parade	93	159	10-14	1
Lap tag	94	160	10-14	1, 4

National Standards for Physical Education *

Standard 1: *Move competently.* Demonstrates competency in motor skills and movement patterns needed to perform a variety of physical activities.

Standard 2: *Understand movement.* Demonstrates understanding of movement concepts, principles, strategies, and tactics as they apply to the learning and performance of physical activities.

Standard 3: *Participate regularly.* Participates regularly in physical activity.

Standard 4: *Achieve fitness.* Achieves and maintains a health-enhancing level of physical fitness.

Standard 5: *Behave responsibly.* Exhibits responsible personal and social behavior that respects self and others in physical activity settings.

Standard 6: *Value activity.* Values physical activity for health, enjoyment, challenge, self-expression, and/or social interaction.

* Standards developed by the National Association for Sport and Physical Education (NASPE, 2004); italicized summary points added.

About the Author

Steven Henkel received his B.S., M.S., and Ph.D. degrees at the University of Wisconsin-Madison. He taught physical education four years in the public schools, and five years at the University of Wisconsin-Madison. Steve is a professor at Bethel University in St. Paul, Minnesota, where he has taught for 25 years, along with directing the teacher licensure program in Physical Education.

Passions of Professor Henkel include promoting motor skill development, creative movement, self-esteem, and developmentally appropriate games for children and youth. He has led AWANA and Vacation Bible School programs in the local church, served as a resource for Christian home educators, and coached youth sports. Steve lives with his wife in Arden Hills, Minnesota, where they raised three sons.

Other selected works by Steven Henkel:

Henkel, S. (2010). Integrating active games with other subjects. Cottage Grove, MN: MGB Printing.

Henkel, S. (2008, contributing author). Concordia Physical Education Curriculum Guide.

Henkel, S. (2007). Honoring God through sports competition. Journal of Christian Education, 50 (2), 33-43.

Henkel, S. (2002). Creative dramas: Picture the possibilities. Teaching Elementary Physical Education, 13 (6), 23-26.

Henkel, S. (1997). Monitoring competition for success. Journal of Physical Education, Recreation and Dance, 68 (2), 21-28.

Henkel, S. (1995). Games for success: Developing children's character through recreational play. Lanham, MD: University Press.